Raising EBITDA:

The lessons of Nip Impressions®

Volume 5

*Recycling/Regulations/Science/
Stupidity/Unclassified*

by

Jim Thompson

Edited by

Stephen K. Roush

Press Nip Impressions

a creative little subset of

Paperitalo Publications, LLC

Duluth, Georgia, USA

ISBN 9780999123492

This book was compiled from original documents. As such, you may detect slight differences in format from time to time, despite our best efforts to provide a consistent presentation.

Dedicated to my sanity,
provided by the most amazing person I have ever met,
my wife, best friend and love,

Laura Feix

and, just in case this is my last book, I want to mention a
few people that have strongly influenced me in each
decade of my life thus far...

1950's My dear Aunt Doris, Midwestern Traffic Manager,
General Telephone and Anna E. Tomasek, missionary to
Rapaydiya, India
1960's Tom Hopkins, high school buddy and missionary
to Peru
1970's Mr. Phil Harris, my lifelong mentor and best
friend
1980's Mr. Mickey Johnson, now retired from BE & K
Engineering
1990's Mr. Gary Byrd, President, Pratt Holdings
2000's Mr. George Mead, retired Chairman,
Consolidated Papers
2010's Lloyd and Melanie Monroe, wonderfully crazy
missionaries in Panajachel, Guatemala

and special mention to
Mr. Rick Gimpel, who has followed me down more wild
career paths than good sense should dictate, especially
considering he is a Marine Corps veteran.

As of this writing all are still with us except Aunt Doris
(deceased, 2005) and Miss Tomasek (1894-1996). From
Aunt Doris, I have a brass candlestick telephone that I

cherish, and from Miss Tomasek, a rosewood elephant she sent me for Christmas, 1963. I would rather have both these strong women leaders back with us, but for the moment, these inanimate items will have to do.

Other books by Press Nip Impressions, Duluth, Georgia,

USA

On Employment (2004)

The Osage Mill (2005)

The Pulp and Paper Industry: a perspective for Wall Street (2006)

The Lazy Project Engineer's Path to Excellence (2006)

Advertising Arguments 2015 (2015)

Advertising Arguments 2016 (2016)

Personalities in the Pulp & Paper Industry (2017)

(indicates first printing)

Forward

For those of you familiar with my writing, you will take one look at this book and say, "That is just a bunch of old Nip Impressions® columns!" Well, you might not add the "®" but you would definitely exclaim the rest of the previous sentence.

On one hand you would be correct—we have gone back through the archives and served up approximately ten years' worth of columns for you.

However, here is the lesson—when I go out into mills as a general consultant, the lessons of these Nip Impressions® columns are what I use. Of course, I do not use all of them, some are quite silly, yet, these are the root source of my ideas. What you see here is the culmination of forty plus years' experience in sales, management and technology in the pulp and paper industry.

And EBITDA? Hopefully, you know this is an acronym for Earnings Before Interest, Taxes, Depreciation and Amortization, in other words, the numbers we operators can control before the finance department employs their magical tricks.

I chose it, "Raising EBITDA," for the title because one of my long term consulting clients raised their EBITDA by roughly 60% in two years recently. Yes, markets were friendly, but I would like to think I had a teeny, tiny part in their success. And, fortunately, they agree. I used nothing but what I know and what I know is here.

I never try to describe my expertise as being a technology specialist. First, I am just not that smart. Second, technology problems probably come in fifth on a list of five things causing failing pulp and paper mills today.

This was not always true. When I was a youngster in this industry, all markets were still growing and technology developments were blossoming. Since then, the environment, internet and public perception have moved to the forefront in our business. In this new world, it is easy to become befuddled and take one's eye off the ball. The Nip Impressions® columns have been a personal centering device for thousands over the years. Now you can have them on your desk, printed on real paper, ready to be consulted a moment's notice, even during a power outage! And there are a couple of power outages mentioned within these covers.

Be safe and we will talk next week,

Jim Thompson
Duluth, Georgia USA

Table of Contents

x

Recycling

A Tale of Two Porches (with apologies to Charles Dickens)

September 2003

I have been recently rebuilding the front porch on our home in Duluth, Georgia. This started out as an architectural/cosmetic project but has turned into much more. The other night, while showering after yet another evening under the joists of what used to be our front porch, a thought struck me. Looking in some old pictures I had from my childhood, I found a crisp Black & White 35mm picture of me nailing away on another front porch in Ohio. It was 1953, I was three, and my Dad and I (probably of not much help) were replacing some old tongue and groove porch flooring that had rotted away.

Fast-forward fifty years. Part of the current project is to replace a floor made of pressure treated deck boards with one that more nearly resembles the tongue and groove porch floors of old. In addition, I am replacing "stick built" square columns with more classic round columns complete with accompanying doodads of cast polymer.

The remarkable thing in comparing these projects is the choices of materials. The new columns are cast fiberglass and the new floor, designed to look somewhat like the tongue and groove floors of old, is recycled plastic grocery bags and soda bottles. These new materials will not rot, be virtually maintenance free and are economical in initial purchase. Remarkably, the materials they are made of, in some cases, did not even exist fifty years ago (a floor of recycled grocery bags in 1953 would, I fear, had quite a papier-mâché look about it and not been very durable).

Thus, the dilemma of our cellulose-based industries today, be the end material solid wood or paper. We simply have not kept up with innovators who are customer-focused and customer-driven in the pursuit of enterprise opportunity and viability. In the case just cited, the floor in particular is an ironic example. Not only is the flooring a superior replacement for a wood product, it is made out of another product, plastic grocery bags, that replaced another paper product twenty years ago.

Our only hope in the faltering sectors of our industry is to go back to the lab, dissect cellulose to its basic components, employ top marketers to discern what the public wants and will buy, and transform our businesses to manufacture those products from the basic building blocks. If the current players will not do this, others will rise up to do so. Cellulose is just too plentiful, renewable and valuable to ignore.

By the way, if you are ever in southwestern Ohio (site of the first porch in this story—Troy, Ohio) you may want to enjoy a fine meal in the Dickens Room at the Golden Lamb in Lebanon, Ohio. This inn and restaurant, purportedly the oldest in Ohio, hosted Charles Dickens when he was touring the United States. His only complaint was that the proprietor was a teetotaler and no alcohol was to be found on the premises.

And, speaking of grocery bags, small children still suffocate every year playing with them and other plastic bags. Please make sure you do not contribute to such tragedy by properly handling your used plastic bags. We will talk next week. ##

Carbon Sequestration and Recycling

Week of 20 Mar 06

A friend of mine reported that at a conference last fall in Asheville, North Carolina (the Southern Roundtable on Sustainable Forests, see http://www.srs.fs.usda.gov/srsf/), Dr. Chad Oliver of Yale University was speaking on carbon sequestration through the building of wood framed homes. Dr. Oliver has been speaking on this subject for a number of years. Others have also taken up the idea of wood as a viable method of sequestering carbon, in fact, I remember reading an article in "Forbes" a number of years ago that discussed the idea of just raising trees, chopping them down and burying them as a way to take excess carbon out of the atmosphere and put it back where we got it (as we extracted oil, natural gas, peat and coal).

This idea may give our environmental advocate friends a bit of heartburn, but I think perhaps there is an interesting idea that is even more provocative. If it is logical that harvested trees, if used in manners in which they are not consumed in some sort of oxidation process so that they can trap and hold carbon, then what about pulp and paper? Does not pulp and paper have the same beneficial attributes? Does not a piece of paper represent the entrapment of some small amount of carbon?

Now, if one assumes all the above to be true, let me take you to another step: which has less future effect on the overall environment—a 3,000 square foot house (we'll assume that represents about 30,000 cubic feet of space) or a solid block of used paper or pulp 31 feet on a side (about the same volume). After all, the large block of used paper does not consume food, energy, gasoline, require education, and all the other demands that the occupants of the house will require. In fact, if we take that cube of paper and place it in a modern landfill and seal it securely, will it not sequester carbon, a lot more carbon, than the house of the same cubic volume?

Of course, I am conveniently ignoring that the occupants of the house must live somewhere—it is not as if they do not occupy this house, they will cease to place demands on society. My point is simply this—this carbon sequestration argument serves to show that we are not close to understanding environmental impact in a holistic sense. Each action has so many ramifications and the entire subject is so new (let's call it 100 years old) that we still know very little.

I would not be surprised if 200 or 300 years from now, the people of that age look at our first feeble attempts at understanding environmental impact with the condescending rearward view we attach to the Salem witch trials or the Catholic Church's attacks on Galileo for daring to say the Earth was not the center of the universe.

So what is the lesson for today? I think it is important for us to understand our ignorance and to reduce the rhetoric of judgment that is pervasive in the world today as pertains to environmental matters. Yes, we are aware there is a problem, and yes, the Earth's ability to absorb humankind's exhaust—gaseous, liquid, or solid, is not limitless. However, the extent and solutions to the problems are not yet known, despite the shrill rhetoric of so-called experts.

For safety this week, let's talk about exhaust. I have known the grown child of at least one person in our industry that was fatally overcome by carbon monoxide while tuning a race car in a closed garage. This silent killer is present in many places.

Be safe and we will talk next week. ##

Recycling, the last frontier

Week of 19 Nov 07

In most countries, the recycling rate is stuck in the 60 to 75% range. There is a reason for this—we have been unwilling to touch garbage, the location of much of the rest of recyclable paper.

Now, if you have been reading my thoughts for a long time, you will know I am not a rabid recycler; the world is not running out of landfills or places to develop landfills (there are a couple of US states that I think would serve quite well as landfills, for instance). When such hysteria

started a decade and a half ago, I coined a word for it—
"irrercyclaphobia"—the fear of not recycling.

Our motivations for recycling now are based on a real economic need—fiber. We are running out of places to grow industrial trees. This need is not going away soon, for as societies around the world continue to develop they need more paper products and more paper products require more fiber. We are seeing this most acutely in the recycled fiber available for manufacturing linerboard and medium (fluting) —the quality of recycled fiber available for these grades decreases every year.

So why don't we recycle the fiber in garbage? I think it is because we haven't tried, not because of technological barriers. It appears that we are short perhaps only one or two developments from doing this. The major development required is a substitute for the plastic garbage bag (so that this large piece of plastic is kept from the recycling stream). Here last week, I mentioned how favorable the ratio of liquid packaging board cost has become to the cost of oil, used for many plastics. This favorable cost ratio should, on its own, help motivate the development of a recyclable paper garbage bag. A paper garbage bag will probably be made from unbleached tissue, for it needs lots of x and y tensile strength, almost no z strength and it must be pulpable. The sanitary tissue makers have been working on these attributes for fifty years or more, developing materials with not only the correct tensile strength properties but with just the right amount of wet strength to maintain temporary physical functionality but then disintegrate under the right conditions.

Now, if we take our collected garbage in our new recyclable bags to a properly designed recycling facility, we can get started. First, it will be sent through a ram style extruder press to remove all the liquids. This will keep soft drinks, grease drippings and so forth out of the recycling system. In fact, this liquid stream may be rich enough to turn into energy but we won't know without testing.

Next we take the dried (through extrusion pressing, not with the introduction of heat) material through a drum pulper. These devices are very effective at separating non-fibrous items (such as broken glass) from the fiber we want. From here on the process is almost routine— screens, cleaners and so forth.

We can heat the fiber to a temperature to kill any bacterial residues. We can clean the fiber satisfactorily to make linerboard and medium. We have a new source of fiber.

I can't resist adding one "political" footnote to this idea. There are some in our industry that see such ideas as ripe for running off and seeking government development money. This idea does not need such largess. There are plenty of large linerboard and medium manufacturers that can take on the development risk on their own or in consortia to develop this quickly without a large cost and without any strings (no pun intended) attached. We have a need (more fiber), a small amount of development work to do (a paper garbage bag) and then the idea is ready for commercialization. Just do it.

Which is what we should always do in safety—just do it.

Be safe and we will talk next week. ##

So what do you really think about recycling?

Week of 13 Apr 09

My derisive comments about certain recycling efforts have apparently led some to think I am opposed to the idea. This is not true. What I am opposed to is stupid or hysterical recycling efforts—hence the term irrercyclaphobia, the fear of not recycling.

When I was a teenager back on the farm, we recycled everything for it was the only way to make ends meet. It was not emotional—it was driven by pure economics. True story: we owned a "1 1/2 Ton" 1953 GMC Truck. Sometimes such trucks are called "bob trucks." They are bigger than pickups, but are not semis (lorries to Europeans). This one had a twelve foot long bed and would hold about 200 bushels of grain. One fall night, dad was driving it from one of our farms to another, loaded down with soybeans he had just harvested. Coming up a long hill, he twisted off the crankshaft, destroying the engine. What to do?

We found in the classifieds in the paper, a 1952 Chevrolet pickup, beat up but running, for which the owner wanted $80. This was cheap, even in those days. Since Chevys and GMCs had essentially the same drive train, we pulled the engine out of the pickup and put it in the big truck—it took one afternoon. But this is not the end of the story. We had a trailer with a rotten wooden bed. I took the bed off the pickup and put it on the trailer frame. Then I stripped everything else off the pickup frame, built a wagon bed out of lumber from a house we were tearing down and put it on the running gear. With a little welding, a hitch was added and steering was converted to wagon style. We had a new wagon. I took the old cab and fenders off the pickup and put them in a ditch where we were experiencing erosion in the pasture—an approved way to handle erosion in those days. Look what we did with a worn out pickup that cost only $80.00—now that is smart recycling. We did not call it recycling—it was just so obviously the right things to do. By the way, when I would get done working on this project each day, I would clean my greasy hands with the approved solvent used by all mechanics in those days, gasoline (with lead in it, of course). Maybe that's why freshman calculus was so tough!

A few weeks ago, I was sitting in the parking lot at our local post office while Laura went inside to mail a package. I was there about 10 minutes. In one corner of the post office parking lot are recycling containers for phone books, magazines and other such things that are not picked up with our trash. While I sat there, just a random 10 minutes on a random day, four people drove on the lot, did not go to the post office, but stopped at the recycling bins to deposit what could not have been more than 5 pounds total of recyclables. Who knows how far they drove, but the CO_2 emissions from their cars surely negated anything they did by recycling these paltry items. This is dumb recycling.

A number of years ago, when I had a fairly large office, we were working on a recycling project. We engaged a specialist from out of town to help us. When I took her back to the airport to catch her flight home, she chided me for not having recycling bins in our office. I shot back, "drug dealers don't use drugs themselves." She was not happy. That is also no doubt an example of how I convey the wrong message.

The problem as I see it today, is we as human beings cannot have a civilized conversation on recycling (and several other environmental subjects—one of which we will cover next week). For example, had I wandered over to the recycling bins at the post office and tried to have a reasoned conversation with these people about the overall, big picture effect of what they were doing, I'll bet they would have bitten my head off. I imagine I would have been accused of being a heartless fool, not interested in saving the planet.

I must admit, I don't know how we begin to start having reasoned conversations with real, big picture answers in today's world.

If one looks back to World War II in America, one finds a practical, full-blown effort towards recycling. Everything was recycled. One reason, in fact, that old farm machinery, especially tractors and steam engines, are so rare today is that they were melted for scrap to make Liberty Ships in World War II. One can find pictures of school yards in small towns across America in those days piled high with old farm equipment, ready to be loaded on to train cars for the trip to the steel mill.

Recycling in those times had a defined, tangible purpose. Recycling today, being a bit ethereal in its aims leaves the individual with no concrete purpose, and hence, I believe, a lack of practical understanding of what they are doing. Some may want to leave it nebulous like this. Personally, I think the entire process would be better served, and perhaps have an even better outcome for the planet, were it more practically oriented. It remains to be seen if this can ever be accomplished.

Of course, safety is not nebulous. We know if we are injury free or not. We achieve excellent safety records only by being focused on the practical.

Be safe and we will talk next week. ##

Regulations

Stop it already!

Week of 24 Nov 08

I am talking about the proposed bailout of GM, Ford, Chrysler and anyone else who has their hand out. Sorry if I am a bit political and provincial this week and way off the topic of the worldwide pulp and paper industry, but when politics invades manufacturing businesses to the extent that all this bailout talk indicates, it is time to bite back.

It has been no secret that I have been, to put it mildly, uncomfortable with our own industry's efforts to tap government largess over the years, often in the name of research and development or saving obsolete mills. However, the auto industry is making us look like mere amateurs.

It is not out of envy or our own incompetence that I say stop. I say it for there are already time honored ways to handle poorly managed businesses: reorganization or liquidation bankruptcy. The bankruptcy system was designed to purge poor operations with the least disruption. This system works and should be employed with vigor to remove the deadweight of these obsolete companies from the macroeconomic scene. And, don't pay any attention to the scare mongers—they would have you believe these companies and their suppliers in their entirety will fail. Not true—the bankruptcy courts will sort out and reorganize the parts with promise. Yet the scare mongers are indeed out in force. Over this past weekend, if one watched the news shows, the number of jobs affected by the big three moved from an estimated 2 million to 5 million. Just yesterday, I heard a business analyst say 10 million. Obviously, everyone is just guessing—and totally ignoring how many jobs would move to domestic operations of Toyota, Honda, Nissan, BMW and Mercedes were they to fill the vacuum in demand created by the loss of the "Big Three."

What goes unsaid, of course, is that the companies to be saved are those whose workers are represented by the United Auto Workers Union. The other auto companies manufacturing in the United States are doing just fine. Sure, they are having a downturn, but they are not in the position where they are likely to go out of business. Their secret? They have good management.

Now, one could construe that I am anti-union. I am not anti-union, I am anti-inefficient union. I have mentioned a number of times over the years the fatal coal mining accident my grandfather experienced in 1930. I am certain the United Mine Workers Union, putting pressure on owners and the government (for safety regulations), have made sure that an accident as stupid as the one in which my own grandfather was killed is almost impossible today. This is right and good.

Middlemen (I don't know how to say this in a unisex way) anywhere do nothing but add costs without adding value. GM, Ford, and Chrysler have not managed their middlemen—the UAW and their dealers. Now, they, the poor management of these three companies, plus the president of the UAW, are running to their friends in Washington begging for help. The excuse is this: they are too big to fail.

Nonsense. What would happen if the much maligned Wal-Mart showed up in Washington stating they were on hard times and too big to fail? They do have 2.1 million direct employees (and the best performing stock in the Dow Jones Industrial Average this year). They would probably get a bailout, IF they agreed to unionize their stores. Wal-Mart is indeed too big to fail—rural America would be thrown into a depression for sure if Wal-Mart went out of business tomorrow. Yet, I don't think we have to worry, for Wal-Mart is very well managed. This past week, they did say their overall results will be below earlier expectations, but that is because of currency exchange losses, not their basic business. Their success has been, to a large part, due to this: they have eliminated the middleman up and down the retail chain. It has been independently reported that when Wal-Mart comes to a small town, it is like everyone in town received a 10% raise. That is effective management and value creation.

Let's look at governments' attempts to "help" other "industries" over the years. Take passenger train service in the United States. It has been on the dole since about 1970. Service has deteriorated to a point of utter ridiculousness while fares have soared above the costs of an airline flight. Who is going to take a 13 hour, if on time, train ride from Atlanta to Washington, D.C. at 1 1/2 to 2 times the price of a one-hour airline flight? Education is another example. Henry Ford, Andrew Carnegie, John D. Rockefeller, Thomas Edison, Albert Einstein, Woodrow Wilson and J.P. Morgan, the people who set the stage for the prosperity of the 20th Century, went to schools without any federal assistance. The only two people of their stature in our times, Warren Buffet and Bill Gates, also completed their pre-college educations without federal assistance. Now, we complain how poor schools are and think the solution is to pile on more aid.

Money comes with strings and I believe strongly in this principle: he who furnishes the money makes the rules. There is already USD 25 billion allocated to "help" the auto industry make more fuel efficient cars. Honda, Toyota and others seem to make fuel efficient cars without any help. If the goal is to keep GM afloat, I say subsidize the selling price of Corvettes to make them competitive with Toyota Scions. I'll bet they will fly out of the showroom and the sole Corvette plant in Bowling Green, Kentucky will have to expand many times over, bringing many jobs to Western Kentucky. More likely, we'll be able to look at other cars made with government help for our examples of cars designed by Fiat: the Russian Lada (who would have thought someone could take a 1960s vintage Fiat and make it worse?) or the East German Trabant, the first car with body panels made of recycled materials. Isn't that exciting—how green! Most likely Trabant clones are in our future. The Trabant was possibly the worst car ever made—it could only sell in a society without free market choice.

Now despite all my venting above, an example appeared

last week that is the argument of arguments for keeping politicians out of businesses. The Canadian law firm Siskinds, based in London, Ontario, filed a 40 page brief in the Ontario Superior Court in Kitchener last week, proposing a USD 550 million class action lawsuit against AIG under the Ontario Securities Act. If allowed to go forward, this suit on behalf of Canadian investors in AIG will have to be defended and, if lost, will require a payout. And whose money will be used for the defense and payout? The US taxpayers, of course, since we have taken on AIG as a basket case. Expect this to be one of many, many lawsuits in all of the messes with government entanglement that have been established this fall. It is the perfect tort case—who has deeper pockets than the US government?

We have had many pulp and paper facilities fail over the years. Their normal course of failure has sometimes been bankruptcy, a process that has been very healthy. Can you imagine if we would have hit the times we are facing today with the pulp and paper industry of 1995? It would be a complete disaster.

We must stop the handouts, for this reason if nothing else—to keep our great grandchildren from spitting on our graves. For we have already placed our children and grandchildren in debt to cover our foolish ways—must we reach yet another generation or two forward with our terrible legacy?

Safety is nothing to compromise in any business at any time. People become upset when there are rumors their business and livelihood are in jeopardy. As you see your relatives in the upcoming holiday season, those which perhaps work in the auto industry, admonish them to be safe on the job.

Be safe, and we will talk next week. ##

What are carbon credits and what do they do for us?

Week of 16 Feb 09

P.T. Barnum is attributed with saying "There's a sucker born every minute" although, he, as the source of this quote is in dispute. Were he alive today, I suspect he would abandon the circus business and jump into carbon credits and carbon trading.

Carbon credits appear to have their genesis in the Kyoto Treaty and its focus on greenhouse gases. The theory is someone can build a something that produces less carbon emission than some other something and sell the "savings in carbon emissions" to someone else who can't or won't reduce their own carbon emissions. On a formal level, governments recognize this activity and on a retail level, you the individual can buy carbon credits to assuage your guilt for polluting.

So, supposing you want to buy some carbon credits, where do you go? Well, since last summer, JP Morgan has been selling carbon credits obtained from promulgating a new type of cook stove in Uganda. We are not talking about large cook stoves here; we are talking about a device that cost the locals about USD 6.00. It looks like a large tin can with some holes cut in it. However, someone somewhere has figured out that the new cook stoves vs. the old cook stoves (I can't even imagine what they were—a tin can with holes in it seems pretty near the beginning of the industrial revolution to me—Napoleon took tin cans with him on his assault on Moscow, 1812) reduce carbon dioxide emissions by two to three tons per year, a credit JP Morgan can sell for $10 to $15 per ton. And the US government had to bail out the large banks like JP Morgan because they were unprofitable??

I have a better idea, claim carbon credits for all Ugandans killed under Idi Amin's dictatorship in the 1970s, after all they don't produce any carbon pollution any longer.

OK, that was a bit of a rough statement, but I am trying to make a point. The Kyoto Treaty no doubt was trying to produce an honorable solution to what is perceived to be a real problem, anthropogenic pollution. However, there are some major holes in this entire scheme.

First, carbon credits are based on the savings of one activity versus another. From a logical and philosophical point of view, this cannot be measured without an argument. "Savings against what?" is a question of endless debate. For instance, should the Amish earn carbon credits for not using electricity? There are enough Amish that their abstinence from electrical consumption should be a significant matter when it comes to measuring carbon dioxide emissions. If one counters this with, "Well, they have always lived this way, there is no savings" one implies that savings has to be against a certain behavior before a certain date. However, if a windmill farm did not exist and now does, why does it generate credits when the Amish don't? If the Amish vote to use electricity this Sunday and rescind the vote next Sunday are they now eligible?

Methane from animals is considered a big pollutant. Fifty years ago, the whitetail deer population in the United States was at its lows for all times. Through good conservation practices, the deer population has exploded and they have become a nuisance. Should the automobile driver that hits one of these flatulent pests or the hunter that shoots one earn carbon credits? After all, humankind's efforts to restore the deer population could probably be considered a form of anthropogenic pollution. Or maybe we should shoot all the polar bears (or moose, or whales, or...).

And once you solve these thorny problems you have one of audit and accountability. Who says how many new stoves are in Uganda? Who monitors the cooking processes used by the poor housewives of Uganda in order to certify that two to three tons of carbon emissions are saved each year? Perhaps that is where JP Morgan got in trouble—they had to move a Vice President to each village as a monitor and flying in their sushi ate up the profits. Or perhaps cut out the stoves altogether and have the Ugandans eat cereal and give the carbon credits to Kellogg's or Weetabix. One can easily see how silly this becomes.

On a large scale, there is an auditing protocol. The validation process is called the Clean Development

Mechanism according to the United Nations Framework on Climate Change. Grandpa Jim is highly suspicious.

Please note that not once have I said in this column it is a bad idea to reduce one's carbon dioxide emissions. In fact, it is probably a good idea, even if you don't believe in anthropogenic pollution. But, wow, we have got to get the process right. I am highly suspicious the current mess is putting lots of money in some sharpies' pockets without doing anything for the planet.

I am glad no one has (yet) come up with the idea of trading "safety credits"—you know, if you want to be unsafe you buy credits from safe operations to offset your lousy record. Safety is real, it can't be traded away.

Be safe and we will talk next week. ##

The test not taken

Week of 12 Apr 10

One of the excuses for the government oversight of today's businesses and economy is that the modern economy is so technologically complex that it requires more control than in the days when our primary energy sources were horses and humans. This is probably true.

However, one thing that has not kept up with this is the standards for legislators and regulators such an environment requires. They do not have to pass a minimum mathematics and science proficiency tests.

This was driven home last week in an episode in the US Congress where representative Hank Johnson, from here in the Greater Atlanta area, quizzed an Admiral about the possibility of over populating Guam and it "tipping over." This video "went viral" in a couple of days, and if you live in North America and have not seen it, it is because you don't have electricity. Now, Congressman Johnson, a few days later, came out with a statement that he was speaking in metaphors. You watch the video, you decide.

Around the world, assuming you live in a democracy, I would dare say the mathematical and scientific intelligence of elected leaders may be more important in some ways than their political leanings. As far as their political leanings go, it is fairly easy to discern if they are people favoring more government control or less, and you can vote as you see fit. Yet, again, there is no test for technological intelligence and these people make many decisions involving technology.

I would dare say, laws and regulations enacted by technologically ignorant legislators have easily cost billions in lost capital and probably millions of jobs.

And there is another technologically ignorant group that contributes to this disaster—the media. Reporters love to play stories of anecdotes and ignore statistics. Let's take, for instance, power generation safety. How many people have been killed by nuclear power generation activities since it came into use? None. How many people have been killed by coal-powered generation activities this year? Well, in the United States we know nearly 30 coal miners have been killed in Raleigh County, West Virginia this week alone. There are reporters crawling all over these poor people's homes trying to get a unique story. Yet, paradoxically, nuclear power is perceived as "dangerous." I have not seen one connection made between coal mining and electrical generation this week.

Now, before I go any further, my words above sound like I am including all legislators, regulators, and media persons as technologically ignorant. We know there are shining stars in all these categories, it is just that the overwhelming majority seem to be this way.

As far as ways to fix this problem, there are both personal and corporate actions to be taken.

On a personal level, you can certainly quiz all candidates. I would be so bold as to ask them the highest level of math, chemistry and physics they ever took in school. I would also ask them if they have taken a statistics course.

On a corporate level, invite legislators and media people to your operations regularly for informational discussions. Stress these are to be camera-free events , informal sit-downs and walk-thrus. Show them how you do things, the science involved and so forth. You don't have to get to the level of corporate secrets, in fact, they will not tolerate that (they will not give you that much time), but give them an understanding and make them your friends. This can be done.

How will you know you are successful? With legislators it will be when they start calling your management team to sort out a technical question they are struggling with elsewhere. With the media, it will be when, in one of their stories, they do not call a papermachine "a gigantic assembly line." Man, does that one bother me, and I have heard it many times.

When I was a freshman in college, 42 years ago, my roommate and I were discussing politics one day. We decided all politicians should be engineers and scientists. That is probably a bad idea for many reasons, but a little dose of it would not hurt.
In the matter of safety, we do have technology and data—loads of it. Pay attention to your safety technology and act accordingly.

Be safe and we will talk next week. ##

Ban the EPA?

Week of 3 Oct 11

Recently, the debate seems to have been opened on the idea of banning the US Environmental Protection Agency. Recent figures cited claim the EPA wants to hire 230,000 more enforcers and coming regulations will kill another 1.4 million US jobs.

As a survivor of a rare type of cancer partially attributed to the unprotected handling of synthetic fertilizers when I was a teenager, I think I have an authoritative opinion on this subject.

How did we get to the place we are? From the beginning of the Industrial Revolution until the 1960s, at least in the US, industries spewed air and water discharges with near abandon. I have always been of the opinion that if industry had adopted the philosophy that if you make it, you keep it, we would never have gotten to the place we did. In other words, what you do on your piece of property is your business, but do not let it encroach on me—keep all your emissions (an aside, this applies to the noise from that loud stereo you play when you are having a party in your back yard, too—I don't want to hear it). This, for me, comes from my libertarian political stance.

So, essentially, business, through ignorance or arrogance, makes no difference, created a situation so obnoxious and so dangerous that the people, through the government, had to step in. I think when the Cuyahoga River in Cleveland, Ohio caught fire in the 1960s, any citizen who had had doubts about the necessity to regulate industrial discharges changed their mind.

But, as humans often do, we overreacted. The mandates of the EPA, over the years, have become ever more stringent. The national discourse on the subject has been taken up by the paranoid, ignorant of any scientific training. I have mentioned before seeing stock photos of a papermill, discharging evaporated water from machine room fans and captioned with "view of paper mill spewing pollution." The person that wrote that was either ignorant or had a dishonest agenda.

So, you may be shocked when I say this, but I don't think we should do away with the EPA. What I do think we should do is study, or agglomerate studies already done to scientifically ascertain what affects at what levels various pollutants have on human, animal and plant life. Of course, many epidemiology studies have been done, but have they ever been assimilated into a master plan for pollution control? I am not aware of such a plan.

Even President Obama is moving toward slowing down the pace of regulation imposition—he knows it is killing jobs. Yet, every time he does this, all the usual loud suspects tell us what harm this is doing. Their claims are a bit of crying wolf too much. It is time build a master air and water control strategy based on science, not politics. Such a plan should provide an assessment of effects on humans, animals and plants. We are willing to accept some risks—otherwise we would not allow the sale of a product, tobacco, which now carries warnings that essentially say this product may kill you if you use it.

No, we should not abandon the EPA, but we should control it and point out to its acolytes that they are not children or teenagers any longer—it is time to act like responsible adults.

For safety this week, of course, emissions can be dangerous, especially concentrated emissions close to the source. Have you had a safety meeting on gas and liquid dangers lately? Perhaps you should.

Be safe and we will talk next week. ##

Fewer employees

Week of 11 Oct 12

The trend toward fewer employees in our pulp and paper mills started many years ago. It was originally driven by cost and quality. Employees obviously cost money. When computers came along that could adjust various attributes in real time, as opposed to employees monitoring conditions, pulling levers and turning valves, the replacement was inevitable.

Then, employees started costing real money. Accidents led to lawsuits, higher insurance premiums and absenteeism. Pensions, insurance and other government mandates have pushed the burden on employee salaries to nearly 40% in some cases, not counting the risk of employee generated lawsuits. Add to this notification rules about layoffs (in the United States) and the near impossibility to lay off employees (Europe) and you can see why employers look at employees as something to avoid.

So, the drive continues to eliminate employees. What's in the future? We have talked about it here before. Expect centralized control rooms where regionally located expert operators run several machines. At the machine site, there will be junior level operators with limited responsibilities.

Look for clothing companies to expand their service with expert teams that come in to install new wires and felts. Since they will be experts, taking fewer hours to do

27

what you have been doing because they do it every day. They also will not be on your payroll.

The large labor component is still in maintenance. The day is coming when regional, central maintenance shops, owned by your company or an outside firm, will receive large unit ops sections from your mill for refurbishment, much like rolls are rebuilt today. This will take more standardization than today, but it is coming.

What is driving all of this? Two things. The first is the ever more complicated equipment which requires highly trained professionals to operate and maintain. The second is government imposed employee liabilities. From layoff notifications to mandates for time off to take care of newborns, to universal health insurance, the more government mandates, the fewer employees.

Now, don't get me wrong. All of these government protections for employees are nice. But companies being what they are, they are going to work very diligently to reduce these costs, costs that these days frequently only start with the salary. The hidden burden is becoming extraordinarily high.

Here in the United States, the tipping point just may be universal health care. It may not be such a large problem for pulp and paper mills, for most still have fairly generous benefits, but it will affect smaller, peripheral companies that serve the industry.

Productivity improvements have steadily driven industry for decades to make more product with less people. That is how societies achieve a higher standard of living. However, we are moving into a new era now, one where the protection burden afforded employees drives companies to do everything they can to eliminate employees. That's the unintended consequences of a high protection requirement.

For safety this week, less people, on one hand, mean less potential for accidents. On the other hand, those still operating our facilities may have to learn new safety techniques as they interact with robots and other devices.

Be safe and we will talk next week. ##

Big Bad Industry

Week of 19 Nov 12

Our industry, and other heavy industries have done dismal job of keeping the public informed of what we do, how we do it, and the benefits to society. I spoke about this earlier this week over on PaperMoney.

The reality today is that the pulp and paper industry is tightly regulated, closely watched, and by and large a good citizen. No, it has not always been that way, and yes there is still the occasional bad apple today. But for the most part, we are good citizens of the world.

The NGOs, such as Greenpeace, Environmental Defense Fund and others, are in transition, a surprising transition. Let's look at a bit of history. In the 1970s, these organizations and others like them came into being. Personally, I was turned off immediately, for they violated laws to make their points—Greenpeace's illegal boarding of fishing vessels sticks in my mind. Justifying your illegal acts because, in your opinion, someone else is doing an illegal act (sometimes not against real laws on the books, but self-determined "crimes against nature") did not cut it with me. After all, maybe I decide I don't like the color you paint your house, a "crime against vision," and I decide to burn it down. What's the difference?

Nevertheless, in those days, these environmental advocates could be considered forward thinkers. They had a vision, whether you believed it or not, that pollution was taking the world down the wrong path. Their vision was ahead of most others.

Now, however, forty years later, the tables are turned. Most activities at pulp and paper mills are done under BACT (Best Available Control Technology) or MACT (Maximum Achievable Control Technology) without exception. These protocols are written into the appropriate regulations and laws.

This leaves the environmental advocates in a quandary. Their job is finished, they have nothing to do. That means they cannot sustain their business model—who is going to give them money? They don't manufacture anything, they are solely dependent on sympathetic handouts (and, when they have been able to manipulate the system) government funds for their prosperity.

So, they ratchet up the rhetoric. They depend on generations of young people born since the major environmental improvements were made. They don't mind if these new generations get the wrong ideas and equate us to the polluters of the 1970s for it helps them survive. The environmental advocates have become the old fashioned part of the equation, and they don't mind that as long as they can continue the myth of pending disaster.

It is time to call them out. I have mentioned elsewhere appeasement does not work. The real objective of the environmental advocacy groups today is their own survival. They cannot afford to declare a great victory for then their income dries up. They are in a predicament.

For safety this week, consider your personal environment as you do your job each day. There are two dangers here. The first is this: if your job requires you to stay in one place all day, you may become complacent to the dangers around you (and there are dangers everywhere, even in an office). If your job requires you to roam around your facility, there may be dangers in places with which you are not completely familiar. Either way, hazards abound.

Be safe and we will talk next week. ##

Science

Where is the power of the hydrogen ion bond?

April 2005

Now, maybe it is just because I am a dumb old mechanical engineer, but I am puzzled. Last week, a colleague who works in product development in a paper company (yes, despite the naysayers, such people and positions still exist) and I were talking about how other materials, such as plastics, have eaten our lunch for the last twenty or thirty years. Yes, it is so old and oft repeated that it is a cliché, but the line from the movie, "The Graduate" about plastics being the future is, indeed, true (by the way, that line is 37 years old this summer).

When I think back over the life of my career, it does seem that other materials have made great strides in utility, economy and simply great usefulness as compared to the source of our economic succor, the lowly cellulose fiber. Aluminum, despite an economic disadvantage on a price/weight basis as compared to steel, has become ubiquitous and displaced steel in many applications (many far beyond the beverage can and aluminum siding). Plastics continue to proliferate, replacing both paper and glass in packaging applications, while glass has moved on to become a truly high-tech, high-value material in fiber optics and other such applications.

The pitiful response I remember to the plastic milk jug replacing paper cartons was a silly study about sunlight destruction of essential vitamins in milk stored in plastic vs. paper. There were two obvious answers to this problem clear to anyone who had been in a fourth grade science class: (1) add pigment to the plastic and (2) keep your milk in the refrigerator, away from sunlight.

Yet, pulp and paper scientists have always touted that the hydrogen ion bond that is made when two paper fibers join is stronger than the interstitial bonds found in carbon steel. Again, being a dumb old mechanical engineer, I have had to take for granted this is the truth. But if it is true, why have we not been able to use this one single fact of physics to bring more glory and remuneration to cellulose fibers? It seems to me to be one of those good, solid microscopic facts that modern technologists are so good at exploiting.

Some of you will write and tell me it is all the fault of the bean counters who have kept us from doing proper research. Others will blame those greedy stockholders who want their returns now, not in the future. Save your breath--every other industry has bean counters and stockholders of the same ilk as ours. There is something else, fundamental, foundational, that is keeping our fiber from reaching its full potential.

If you are looking for the answer in this brief piece, you will be disappointed, because I do not have an answer. It is time, however, that we figure out a way to find the answer to this problem, and I suspect it will involve new people bringing new ideas to our industry. Last week, for instance, at AF&PA's Paper Week in New York, I heard Ronee Hagen, the new CEO of Sappi's North American operations, speak. She came to our industry a short five months ago from aluminum. She may be the kind of person that can bring us the insights we need. Time will tell.

Meanwhile, you might be a slovenly bureaucrat if--you prepare reports for senior management by starting with the answer you want and building backup that "proves" your   point.
For safety around the mill, focus on ladders this week, please--how they are extended, the footing they sit on, the buddy system to hold the bottoms on higher work. We will talk again next week. ##

Real Science and Creativity

April 2005

A few examples from my other favorite industry this week, served up here to perhaps inspire us and help us understand that there is a future in our own. That other favorite industry, as longtime readers know, is agriculture, an industry whose entire sales model is the open auction. Talk about commodities! That is all these people have to sell.

Here is the level of sophistication we now see in this industry. Most of these items are gleaned from the April 2005 issue of the Ohio Farmer, a tabloid size magazine of 52 pages, 75% of which are advertising.

Eric Berg, a scientist at the University of Missouri, has discovered that stress in pigs leads to PSE pork. PSE is an acronym for meat that is Pale, Soft, and Exudative. This is caused when pigs are moved to processing and are not allowed to have a day or two to "chill out" before slaughter. Stressed pigs apparently have increased temperature, blood pressure and hormones. If slaughtered in this condition, these issues affect the quality of meat resulting in PSE pork. Great research--how can we do research at this level in the paper industry?

High priced gasoline is good for the farm. Ethanol production will consume nearly 1.8 billion bushels of corn this year, up from only 650 million in 2000. The market conditions have nothing to do with agricultural science, but the ability to convert corn to ethanol does. One valuable byproduct, which does have something to do with recent research, is that the solid waste left from manufacturing ethanol is being turned into valuable animal feed.

This hits close to home for us in the paper industry. The National Dairy Council (NDC) has done a study that shows that school children, drinking milk for lunch, consume 18% more milk when it is provided in single serving plastic bottles and not "old fashioned" paper milk cartons. Only 1,250 schools have switched, but the NDC is pushing for widespread adoption in order to increase milk consumption.

One farmer has built his own corn planter because he did not think the ones provided by the equipment manufacturers were big enough. With his, he can now plant 400 acres (162 hectares) per day. Coupled with real-time kinematic GPS auto steer (a method of hands-free driving precise to within 25 mm) in the tractor pulling this unit, he can do many other jobs on his Wi-Fi equipped computer while planting these acres.

On Thursday, I attend the annual meeting of AGCO, a worldwide tractor and farm implement manufacturer headquartered here in Duluth, Georgia. This company has taken old-line companies that were failing and has put them together in a way creating a behemoth. Their most recent acquisition was the old Valmet tractor line from Finland, but they also own White, Oliver, Massey Ferguson, Fendt, Allis Chalmers and other venerable old names. Net sales last year were US$ 5.2 billion, as compared to US$ 3.5 billion the year before. Net earnings per share increased to US$ 1.75 from US$ 1.25. Engineering will be expanded 20% this year and diesel engine manufacturing 50%, all from free cash flow--no new borrowings.

All of these things are happening in an industry solely dependent on selling commodities. The great question this leads to is what is preventing the pulp and paper industry from behaving likewise?

You might be a slovenly bureaucrat if--you are more concerned about the actions of your coworkers than you are about your own.

For ethics this week, consider the tools your employer provides--computer, fax, Internet connection, cell phone and so forth. Do you give any thought to using these for personal business? We will talk next week. ##

Technology Cross Fertilization

May 2005

A couple of weeks ago, this column cited a number of tidbits from the *Ohio Farmer*. The comments and responses were voluminous. Many were curious about the various technologies mentioned.

This got me to thinking about one citation in particular-- the farmer that built the corn planter that can plant 400 acres per day. Of particular interest to me was the math involved, for with his modern equipment, he is exactly placing and recording where each seed is placed. What I got to thinking about was the math behind this--exactly how many seeds is this? Assuming rows on 24-inch centers and seeds 3 inches apart in the rows, he is exactly placing 34,848,000 seeds per day (I will let you do the math to check me). By the way, a corn seed is about as thick as a softwood fiber is long.

Shift to a sheet of paper, A4 in size (210mm x 297mm). If this is 20# bond, it weighs 75.2 gsm. Now, I asked a scientist who is supposed to know these things, "How many fibers are in a gram of paper?" Answer: 16,000,000. So, doing the math again, one A4 sheet of 20# bond contains 75,043,584 fibers (again, I will let you do the math and I am sure you will correct me if I am wrong).

Here is where it gets interesting. We know how to look at

individual fibers, in fact, a number of companies make instruments to do so and at least one of these is available in an online version now. Intriguingly, one sheet of A4 20# only contains nominally twice as many data points (75,043,584 vs. 34,848,000) as the four hundred acres of corn.

Eureka! We are very close to having the computational ability to custom place every fiber in an A4 sheet of paper. Granted, if you used just the veneer of data, it would take twice as long to make one sheet as it does for our efficient farmer to plant 400 acres of corn. However, there is travel time and other such matters involved in the corn planting exercise, i.e., the machinery to place the fibers has to travel much smaller distances to make the sheet of paper than does that used to plant the corn. The key is the ability to handle such a volume of data, the mechanical engineering to place the fibers is relatively trivial (for validation of this triviality, one has only to look at the automated machines the aircraft industry uses to build composites from precisely placed individual strands of graphite).

Concerning the ability to handle the data, following the famous Moore's law of computational power, in about 5 or 6 years maximum, we may have the *computational* capability to manufacture our 20# A4 sheet with exactly placed fibers as fast as we can make it on a paper machine now.

Think what this means--a total revolution in papermaking. Instead of relying on the "perfect randomness" we try to create in forming devices now, we can look at each fiber and place it where we desire in the sheet. We can coat fibers individually with unique additives and control their individual moisture. Sheet properties undreamed of today become routine. No more broke. Paper machines move from analog to digital. Paper machines become small and local, rather than large and distant. We make paper exactly as we want, when we want, and where we want it. It will not be your father's papermaking any more. Who says we are in an uninteresting industry? The best years may be just around the corner.

Now, please do not call this idea "bio" or "nano" anything. I have never seen terms become clichés so fast, unless maybe it was the dot-com thing. From now on, bionanos are those yellow-skinned things I peel, slice and have on my cereal for breakfast.

You might be a slovenly bureaucrat if--you engage in "lazy brain" activities, that is, for example, you don't check your facts before inserting them in and sending them out in a memo.

For ethics this week, consider accountability. When it is time to be accountable for your results, do you accept responsibility for all matters under your control or do you try to blame extraneous conditions for things you can really fix? We will talk again next week. ##

A far-fetched pulping idea...

December 2005

Not one to fear putting forth the perceived crazy idea, I offer the following to the general discussion today about pulping and extraction of valuable other products from trees. What if we could develop a system to pulp in situ, meaning pulp in the forest at the source of the cellulose (trees)?

The agricultural community has moved this way in the last 150 years in the harvesting of nuts, seeds and so forth, starting with McCormick's reaper, which automated the cutting process. After that, for another 80 to 100 years, the gathered stalks with seeds were taken to a central place to have the grain removed. Then in the 1930s, the idea of combining all of these processes into one portable machine took hold--called, appropriately, the combine.

In pulping, we are still stuck at the McCormick reaper stage. The feller-buncher is the equivalent of the reaper, but we still haul the tree, and a bunch of things we don't want (such as dirt imbedded in the bark), to the pulp mill for further processing.

You purists will tell me that I am mixing metaphors, for in grain harvesting, we extract seeds and nuts, not the stalks. And, after all, you will continue, our sugar manufacturing cohorts, who want material in the stem, still haul everything to the sugar mill to extract the juice. All of this is true, but that should not keep us from trying.

Think, if like some science fiction movie, we could approach a tree identified for harvest, insert some sort of probe, and extract everything we want in a process akin to letting the air out of a balloon. Whether we then stored the extractives as a liquid slurry to be further processed elsewhere or continued the process with more components on the same mobile unit, we would have accomplished the first portion of the process with less fuss and muss (read: less labor, energy and environmental effects) than we do now.

What keeps us from doing this? I certainly do not have all the answers--but I have an answer to the first part, and that is dare to dream we can do things another way. Once that barrier is broken, we can move to solving the other problems, which are relatively simple because they have scientific solutions--not psychological ones.

Look at cotton picking. Long after seed extraction was mechanized, cotton picking was still a hand chore. After World War II, some scientists and engineers dared to dream, and developed the cotton picker. The modern cotton picker does the work of 80 people picking cotton by hand, yet until a mere 60 years ago, it was universally accepted that this process could not be mechanized. The same has happened with the harvesting of fruits and vegetables to a lesser extent.

So, if you researchers want something really exciting to work on, leapfrog the current incremental ideas and move on to some truly innovative ways to take our industry to the next level. Otherwise, we will have to wait for our great, great grandchildren to do these things.

This is our last column before the holidays are upon us (Chanukah, Christmas, Kwanzaa, New Year's and perhaps some others) so may I caution you regarding safety around presents and so forth. There are plenty of holidays that personally turn tragic with improper, inexperienced or excited use of new motorbikes, guns and other gifts. Be careful, I selfishly want to keep you as readers and contributors to our great and wonderful industry in 2006! ##

Yet another anniversary, noted with sadness

Week of 17 Jul 06

I remember where I was, that Sunday evening in the summer of 1969. I was in Sawyer Hall, a residence dormitory at the University of Cincinnati. Looking out the windows briefly, my roommates and I noted there was no traffic on the four-lane street—none. We quickly turned back to the little black and white television and watched Neil Armstrong step onto the Moon—it was July 20, 1969.

What we did not know and did not foresee at the time was that we were witnessing the end of an age of technology magic. Sure, there have been many great accomplishments since then, especially in medicine and computing, but July 20, 1969 was the end of the magic that had been going on for 130 years (aside and surprisingly, the most powerful calculating machine used to accomplish a large portion of it was the slide rule).

The magical era was a time when science and technology manifested themselves in ways absolutely dramatic to the lay person. It started with the telegraph. Then in quick succession we had (1) manufactured goods with interchangeable parts, (2) steel ships, (3) breech loading weapons, (4) the typewriter, (5) the telephone, (6) the light bulb, (7) distributed electricity, (8) the automobile, (9) the airplane, (10) widespread indoor plumbing, (11) nuclear energy and then the landing on the Moon—an average of one every 10 years. And, no, I don't put the Internet in this category. Although amazing, it was just not a big enough leap from the day before we had the Internet until the day after to be qualified as the kind of advancement I am speaking of here.

We take all these things for granted today. To understand how big a "wow factor" they were in their time, I recall an actor dying in the early 1990s at nearly 100 years of age. In his final years, he was asked about the most important innovation in his decades in the theater. His one word answer: "electricity." In fact, the Savoy Theatre in London was the first public building in the world to be illuminated by electricity (October 10, 1881). It had its own 120 HP Siemens steam engine and generator, which apparently caused a flicker in the lights due to a slight acceleration/deceleration of the crankshaft as the engine went through its power stroke/exhaust stroke cycle (perhaps the flywheel was undersized).

What concerns me now is how the lack of a "wow" goal by humankind is potentially affecting the younger generations, especially in the highly developed countries.

What seems to be happening is that we are turning into a population akin to the natives of the island of Nauru in the South Pacific. This island's deposits, rich in phosphate mixed with guano, are highly prized as a source of fertilizer. In fact, the island is so small, the mineral deposits so large, that no one has to work. They just live off the proceeds of the mineral sales. This has led to widespread obesity, alcoholism, automobile fatalities and extraordinary suicide rates, for the natives are required to do nothing in order to live prosperously. Sound familiar?

So, our young people do not see in the media or our lives a large, nearly impossible goal being tackled by the older generations. I hate to say this, but at the risk of sounding like a puritanical preacher, it seems to me we are not challenging the younger generations by our own example. We have run out of "wows" and need one desperately. And while some major issues, such as caring for the environment, are certainly very important, they do not have the pizzazz of the kinds of goals of which I speak. Additionally, such goals are filled with politics and arguments—is there global warming or is there not? Going to the Moon or flying were much simpler goals— you either succeeded or you failed.

So, 37 years ago this coming week, we lost our magic. What are we going to replace it with? What kind of goals can we find to cast in front of the rising generation to inspire them to exceed the accomplishments of those in the past? How can we in the pulp and paper industry contribute to such goals? How can we as individuals?

Back to the Moon, for a moment. There was a great movie about the landing made in 2000, starring Sam Neill. It did not get much exposure in the United States, but was well-received in Australia, for it portrayed a critical role Australia played in all of us seeing Neil Armstrong stepping on the Moon. It is called "The Dish" and if you have not seen it, I highly recommend it.

For safety this week, let's resolve to always be positively excited about this topic--safety. We must never let our guard down when it comes to safe actions and accident prevention. We will talk next week. ##

Does value lie at the microscopy level?

Week of 11 Dec 06

A cellulose fiber is a beautiful thing to behold. It has many wonderful qualities, including smoothness, translucence, and so forth. So, then, why do so many of the products we make from this fiber look like crap?

We were talking last week about our noble competitors, plastics. And with plastics, films, and foils, many products can be made that are pleasing to the eye, the sense of touch, and even smell. (Although the spoilsports are telling us that the brand new car smell is bad for us).

It seems to me that if we want to exploit new nanotechnologies, we would find ways to combine cellulose fibers in a way that raises their functionality beyond just utility. Papers of colors that shimmer in the light, all accomplished by the way we lay each fiber next to the last one come to mind.

Often today, our products look like a toothpick dipped in white glue and then rolled in a batch of dry cellulose fibers. This is not pleasing to the customer and is tolerated only because someone has not developed something better.

Take the lowly field corn plant. From this we get syrup, a beautiful syrup that is sweet, delicious, and for this old farm boy, an irresistible symphony when combined with good old white bread slathered in peanut butter. The Four Seasons has not a dessert to trump this.

Now, you know I am on a kick to make active products, not passive ones. So, let's say with my nano construction, I am able to make an ear swab-like device, nano assembled, that takes my temperature whilst I clean my auditory canals. Just a glance and the sheen it reflects tell me if everything is OK. I find this a useful gadget and I can make it all from cellulose (sorry, cotton). We lack only ideas.

For safety this week, we will reinforce your mother's admonishment about cotton swabs in your ears. She told you no, never, I say be careful.

Be safe and we will talk next week. ##

Paper Airplanes

Week of 9 Nov 09

It seems like UAVs have become ubiquitous in my thinking recently. A "UAV" is an "Unmanned Aerial Vehicle" and they are very popular with the military these days, as well as in some other applications. (Grammar note: "an UAV" just does not sound right, so we'll use "a UAV" here).

This past Friday, I was at Miami University in Oxford, Ohio, where I serve on the Advisory Council in the School of Engineering and Applied Science. Various research projects were showcased to the group, and there were those UAVs again. Still having Attention Deficit Disorder after all these years, I got to daydreaming about how we might use these in pulp and paper manufacturing. Some of my ideas follow and I'll probably expand on these over the next few months in The Thompson Private Letter.

First, it occurred to me these would be quite handy around paper machines. One could have whole coveys of these (each no bigger than a tennis ball, some as small as a golf ball), roosting in a recharging station like pigeons in a pigeon loft, sort of a 3-D "Roomba" experience (the robot vacuum cleaner that always finds its way back to the recharging station and plugs itself in). These little UAVs, some specialized, some generalized, could fly about the paper machine hall at the direction of the operators in the control room, on pre-programmed paths or at the direction of others (more about others in a minute). They could be programmed so that some are in flight and some are recharging all the time. They could have all kinds of sensors and visual cameras. For instance, linked to data logging systems, they could hover near recent locations of paper breaks and zoom in for a close look as soon as a break occurred. They could fly in dryer hoods, press sections and hover over the wire for an up close look at the wet line or even a nip.

Around the winder, specialized UAVs could routinely check the slitters and sample the air for dust, discovering a slitter blade is dull and needs changing before it is even noticeable to humans.

If a valve stuck or a motor seemed to be overheating, operators or maintenance personnel could dispatch a UAV to the scene to visually check out the problem. No matter if the location is high in the room or the atmosphere is unpleasant or unsafe for humans.

All of these capabilities could also be used by others-- specialists sitting somewhere and monitoring all the machines within the corporation or possibly specialists working for an equipment supplier. They could zoom in with specialized and visual UAVs, analyzing problems without ever having to go to the millsite. They could simultaneously look at similar conditions on two or more machines thousands of miles apart.

Sensors that could detect a human in danger (sensitively tuned to human trauma signals) could instantly dispatch special UAVs to the scene of an accident and give an immediate report to EMTs and off-site Emergency

Responders so they would know the details (temperature, heart rate, breathing status and so forth) before they ever arrived, thereby helping in the critical few minutes after an accident happens. Another way to sensitize the UAVs to potential human danger would be to have all employees wear Wi-Fi linked proximity sensors that alert the UAVs any time a human is too close to machinery, so they could be on the scene almost immediately, perhaps intervening with the human before an accident even happens, getting the human's attention by "dive-bombing" like a bee or wasp.

In the woodyard, UAVs could regularly check wood piles for moisture, delivering data from many sampling points to data logging algorithms wirelessly. Same in recycled fiber yards. In powerhouses, UAVs could safely look for high pressure steam leaks high up in boiler houses without endangering humans. UAVs could routinely survey pipe racks for leaks or routine maintenance throughout the mill.

In warehouses, UAVs could take a physical inventory every shift.

After a truck or railcar is loaded, but before the doors are closed, a UAV could fly over the entire load (in the narrow space between the top of the load and the top of the truck or railcar), recording its condition completely as a permanent record for future freight damage claims.

Sophisticated UAVs should be able to maneuver inside barking drums and drum pulpers (after all, people fly in airplanes through hurricanes). Lime kilns may be a bit warm, however.

Within 15 years, I'll wager, a modern mill will have a fleet of 100 or more UAVs doing all sorts of tasks that help the mill control costs, make better quality products and improve safety. Why can I say this with such certainty? I have described nothing here that does not already exist in its separate and disparate parts. In fact, if you want to make a crude one now, just take a hobbyist's radio controlled helicopter and hang a streaming Wi-Fi compatible camera on it (you can build this for less than $500). After that, it is just miniaturization, software and refinement. Untethering sophisticated sensors and allowing them to go where they are needed makes so much sense. It is just as plain as day to me that this will happen soon--hope I get to see it.

Just think what we could do more safely with UAVs--check or sniff tanks, observe rotating machinery and other matters that humans have to do in close proximity now. But in the meantime, we need to be safe and live to see the day when these dangers are reduced by UAVs.

Be safe and we'll talk next week. ##

FarmVille

Week of 30 Nov 09

FarmVille is a game on Facebook. If you are not familiar with Facebook, I would be very, very surprised; for I have already been shocked by my Luddite acquaintances who are there (I think their kids dragged them there to see pictures of their grandkids).

I am going to end this column with a direct application to the pulp and paper industry, but please indulge my wanderings for a minute or two.

FarmVille was launched last June. By October, it had 54 million players around the world. Despite my horrible reputation for messing up simple math here on Nip Impressions, I am going to take the plunge again. If these 54 million spend only 15 minutes each per day on this game, this is equivalent to building the Great Pyramid of Giza (also known as Khufu or Cheops) in about two months. I'll confess to spending at least 1/2 hour per day on it.

My wife and her brother, when I told them about this addiction, told me to "get a life." This was while they were sitting watching a ballgame on TV--enough said.

FarmVille has many, many lessons about capitalism, management, friendship, helping others. If one really thinks about it, it is quite deep, for the hidden rules that have been set up encourage one to act in certain ways. So far, it has been "sweetness and light"--everything turns out nice. However, it is constantly under development, so I expect (and hope) it someday has floods, droughts, pestilence, tax collectors, environmental regulators and so forth, just like real life.

The real life piece that it brings is that it links people one may know but may have not talked to in years. You have "neighbors." One of my "neighbors" is a cousin I have not seen since 1962. A couple of others are cousins I have never seen before (in my family, there are so many scattered cousins, they can hardly be counted). Others are friends from across the years from wildly divergent geographic locations (one is an engineer in Egypt who happens to be a native of India).

FarmVille is not the only game on Facebook. There are many, many others, with equally plentiful and devoted followers. These games are all being developed by a company called Zynga, in San Francisco, California. Their games also work on iPhones.

Here's where the pulp and paper industry comes in. Back in the mid-1990s, I had a vision of an online pulp and paper mill simulator, where we could all play around the clock. My idea was to have managers, operators, technical people, maintenance and so forth. I thought it would be a great learning experience. I presented it to the senior management of a large technical organization on 3 Oct 1995 (I remember the date, for it was the date O.J. Simpson was acquitted). They said, "Great Idea!" and wished me well. I spent years trying to find volunteers to help put it together to no avail.

Zynga could do this. It would probably have to be a general process plant game in order to attract enough players, but that is OK. I have already written to them and begged them to consider this. They, of course, think I want a fee.

(Not that a fee would not help put bread on the table around here.) I do not--I just want to see it built and operating.

To help with this project, what I would like for you to do is this. If you think such a process plant game would be instructional, informative and a good training tool, let Zynga know. Send them an email at Businessdevelopment@zynga.com. Use your own words, or use these:

"Dear Zynga:

"Please develop a game that simulates the operation of a process plant with pumps, valves, pipes, vessels, boilers and so forth. If you can make it a pulp mill that would be great."
Pass this column around and get everyone you know (in industry, academia, your kids) to write to them, if you please. We may finally get an around the world, 24/7 simulator we can all use.

Of course for safety this week, it is inevitable we point out the danger of too much time in front of the computer. Make sure your work place is ergonomically friendly.

Be safe and we will talk next week. ##

Innovative uses for paper and paperboard

Week of 19 Apr 10

In the past few months, this writer has been attempting to inject some reality into your thinking about the future of paper, especially paper used for communications. Admittedly, this has not been a cheerful conversation.

However, there are recent reports with some hope. You will notice, that like all such matters, the issue is one of economics, in this case micro-economics related to improved margins in certain businesses.

The Economist, in its 10 April 2010 edition shows several ways paper and paperboard products may play a role in the future. In an article titled "Loving Touch" which appears on page 67 of that issue, several attempts at enhancing physical products are pointed out. First up: "Fortune" magazine began printing on higher basis-weight paper in March in an attempt to distinguish itself and stand out from the crowd (good job, paper salespeople!). Other print magazines are trying similar ideas.

The article goes on to say what is happening in music CDs. Despite downloads, many music companies still experience their highest sales volume in CDs. The most interesting concept pointed out in this article is about this very subject. Music purveyors are learning there is a multi-tier market for CDs--the plain one and the upscale commemorative set. What is in an upscale commemorative set? A higher end package (think liquor or perfume) and perhaps a poster or other memorabilia (all paper, of course).

Think of all of this as a designer driven media experience. So far, at least, while electronic media is providing a fantastic, animated and multi-hued 2-D experience, that experience lacks the archival, upscale experience of a 3-D package one can display on a shelf.

Here we are competing with pottery, metals and other materials people proudly display in their bookcases. If we can evoke the feel of richness, we can certainly compete on material costs.

Way back in 1970, my father was working in the prototype shop at Kenner Toys in Cincinnati, Ohio. One of the innovations at that time was something called the SSP toy car. It used a flywheel and rack and pinion system to go really fast. But it was innovative in another way, too: it was the first time they made a product where the packaging cost more than the product in the package. The complete ensemble was a huge hit. Later, when they got the contract from Lucas Productions to hurry Star Wars figures to market by Christmas 1977, they actually succeeded in selling empty paper boxes (they could not get some of the figures to market in time for the holiday, so they shipped empty boxes with a certificate that could be redeemed the following February for the actual toy). Redemption rates were less than 5%.

So, perhaps modern purveyors of goods are rediscovering the value high quality packaging and paper can add to retail products. This is a bright path forward for certain grades.

Again, the key is to create a high value experience with materials less expensive than the competition. If you can do that, you can win.

For safety this week, some of the most high value paper you have in your mill are your safety procedures. Reading and following them can result in a fantastic return in safe and healthy employees.

Be safe and we will talk next week. ##

Honest Science

Week of 3 Jan 11

In case you haven't noticed what has been going on in the Northern Hemisphere for the past couple of weeks, Mother Nature has thrown a couple of huge snowballs at the Global Warming, aka, Climate Change, Scientists, their funders, and their acolytes. It has been amusing, to read all the explanations of why the blizzards and record low northern temperate and tropic zone temperatures fit perfectly with the global warming scenarios. Most of these explanations have the Jet Stream doing back flips in order to fit the outcomes directly observable by people in North America, Europe and Siberia. Other quotes point out that global warming scientists in 2000 said that children in England, by 2010, would almost never see snowfall, global warming was so severe and so imminent. Where are those people hiding now?

Don't bother to write me letters telling me how global warming in the big picture is still a viable scenario. From now on, I'll look out my window to form my judgments on the climate. One could possibly say all climates are local, as well as all pollution. In fact, I will say it: if I can see or measure it and it is something that is not where it is supposed to be (oil in a river, smoke in the air, the music in your automobile so loud it permeates my automobile), that is pollution. Otherwise, leave it alone.

How did we get where we are with the silly climate scenarios? We have created boatloads of scientists that want to do nothing but continue the science experiments they were doing in secondary school chemistry and physics classes. They are not brave enough to work for industry and be accountable for the outcomes of their experiments—they must work for governments (through grants), who are the only entities that will fund them. And, like comedians, who have to tell raunchier and raunchier jokes in order to get an audience reaction and continue their livelihood, these scientists must conjure up bigger and bigger outrageous stories in order to keep the money flowing. The governments like this, for the projected outcomes allow government bureaucrats the opportunity to exercise control over industry. The acolytes are on board simply because they are paranoid.

Scientists working for industry are accountable for making the invoice printer spin, not writing farfetched stories to obtain more grant money. They and their managers ultimately have to be honest about what they are doing for if they are not, their source of livelihood, the company for which they work, will fail due to their poor results. Scientists funded by grants do not have this accountability.

These conditions have nearly ruined the formerly great research institutions in the pulp and paper industry. When the scientists could not turn out results the member companies could use to spin the invoice printer, member company funding dried up. The scientists turned to government grants, where funding is decided based on political policies, not whether or not the industry will be improved. Hence, today, we have many so-called pulp and paper scientists engaged in producing results for governments which fund them based on the policies the governments see fit to promulgate. Meanwhile, collaborative research of benefit to the industry has nearly disappeared.

Stated another way, honest science spins the invoice printer, politically funded science, at its best, does not spin the invoice printer and at its worst, slows or stops the invoice printer. These are the conditions we find ourselves in today. In order to compete in today's world, we must turn this situation around quickly.

For safety this week, if you are in the northern hemisphere, for goodness sakes, take appropriate safety precautions in the cold. Hypothermia and frostbite are closer than you think.

Be safe and we will talk next week. ##

Dimensions

Week of 25 Jul 11

Of all the problems I have seen in 41 years in this business, dimensional errors in construction projects ranks No. 1 among internal problems (misjudging markets is far and away No. 1 when you take into account matters outside the mill fence). Yes, programming goes wrong, employee relations can suffer and a myriad of other problems can affect your business' performance, but dimensioning errors stand head and shoulders among big problems that should be easily solved or never occur in the first place.

After all, most dimensioning problems are simple arithmetic. The most complicated versions involve a bit of geometry or trigonometry (as when something is lined up and bolted to another unit at an angle). None of them involve calculus.

Why are these such a problem? In my early days, the excuse was the difficulty in taking such dimensions from existing installations, for if you did not hire an alignment company to come in and do it, the typical engineering department did not have the means or skills to do so. I really think the problem was mostly laziness and lack of attention to detail. Today, there are all sorts of fancy measuring instruments that are relatively inexpensive and easy to operate, yet problems still abound. Again, attention to detail seems to be lacking.

In some cases in the past, the sheer amount of details and the opportunity for a routine amount of human error was a problem. I ran a group early in my career that did what is called detailing steel. This is taking the structural design drawings, often for a high rise building, and turning them into what are known as shop drawings. When this was manual work, as it was up until the mid-1980s, the chance for error was huge and expensive. It was not unusual for a 50-story building to have 20,000 bolt holes that had to match up. The most conscientious team you could put together had an error rate of 2%, or 400 holes (the tolerance on the whole building was 1/8" off--more than that it was a missed hole). The backcharges in those days were $50 per hole for missed holes, or, in this example $20,000. The entire project had a gross sales price to the detailer of $50,000 (this was and is all competitively bid). Hence, backcharges were 40% of the contract price, the best you could do. Thank goodness, computers have largely taken over this tedious task.

But the same thing happens in machine erection and especially in rebuilds. Most engineers tend to look down their noses at the dimensions (makes no difference if they work for the mill, equipment builder or engineering company), after all, this is mere arithmetic. Reader, it is the most important arithmetic in your professional life. It deserves extreme attention to detail.

Several years ago, in the representative side of our business, we chose to resign an account due to this problem. We were tired of making excuses for the supplier we represented to irate customers. In fact, it is hard to make excuses when you agree with the customer 100%. We also felt it was hurting, or had the potential to hurt, our reputation. No one needs business like that.

So, no matter your role, engineer, supplier, production, or anything else, pay attention to dimensions and fit. It is one of the greatest opportunities to save money for your company that exists today.

Safety can be impaired when items don't fit. The pressure to get back up and running can cause people to take shortcuts that should not be taken, resulting in risky conditions. Don't do it.

Be safe and we will talk next week. ##

Stupidity

Welcoming Sights

September 2005

Spent the first four days of last week making sales calls at 10 mills in six states. I thoroughly enjoy these trips to the field--a chance to meet new people, see old friends and so forth.

One thing has struck me over the years and was driven home in this intense trip last week. It is this: entering a mill is a fairly unfriendly experience and one does not often feel welcomed, especially if they are a salesperson. Some of this is understandable, and a good salesperson will walk through stinky, gooey material waste deep to reach a prospect, but it does not reflect well on mills or their management. And, besides, sometimes someone you really want to impress, such as the boss from headquarters or perhaps a customer, is forced to enter the same way.

Let us start with the phone systems. One mill I was attempting to set up appointments with has, on their phone system as of August 23, 2005, the following prelude at the beginning of their general number message: "Please listen carefully as we have new telephone options as of July 1st, 2003..." It will not surprise you that I have made seven attempts to meet with this mill's purchasing department in the last couple of years and have never gotten past the guard shack, despite calls to set up appointments in advance every time. Very impressive.

Another mill had a nicely painted sign directing all visitors to the administration building. Once there, the former reception area was found closed up and a hand scrawled sign said, "All visitors report to the main gate." This is a good half-mile away, and near where the sign was directing all visitors to report to the administration building. Very Impressive.

In most mills, you have us lowly salespeople enter through the guard shack these days. Until last week, I kept wandering into these places and feeling like they were vaguely familiar, not to each other, but to something somewhat remote. It finally hit me--most of them have the charm, décor, ambiance and housekeeping of a convenience store restroom. The only thing missing is the Hygeia dispenser.

Like it or not, you are sending an overpowering feeling with these first impression facilities and it is not just their odor. As a salesperson, there is obviously a strong message that we are not a valuable member of your team--just sell it to us cheap, quality does not matter. You are also sending a strong message about yourself: that details are not important, that quality is not important, that high standards are not important. If one were not a professional, after passing through such an experience, it may be tempting to think, "I can sell these fools any old junk, for obviously quality is not important to them."

You may be a slovenly bureaucrat if you do not check the "reason for visit" column in your sign-in register regularly and especially after a visit from the headquarters management team. You will be surprised what they write in that column. Sometimes it is even things like, "If anyone reads this within 24 hours of my visit and calls me, I will send them $100." I have seen it happen. I also heard the CEO who did that say he had never had to make a payout.

For safety this week, make sure your guards are vigorously enforcing the use of PPE (personal protective equipment) by your visitors. We will talk next week. ##

Mystery Solved--why students are not enrolling in pulp and paper educational opportunities

October 2005

It is simple--because they can't find the #@!##&@ page on any given university's website!

I had occasion this past week to look up several pulp and paper schools on the Internet. I had an advantage--I actually knew which universities have pulp and paper schools. However, even armed with this knowledge, try going to most universities' websites and find the pulp and paper school. Impossible. It is also impossible to find any link on these sites that indicates scholarships might be available.

So, imagine you are a bright 16 year old living in a rural area. Your science teachers and math teachers tell you that you have real promise. Your family is not wealthy; in fact, your family doesn't even own a computer, let alone have web access at home. You have heard from some neighbors that the big pulp mill 20 miles down the road has some highly trained scientists. Your family is not educated--your dad works as a laborer at a local warehouse. You want a good career, but want to live near home. Pulp and paper sounds like the place to be. You go to your high school's library, wait your turn to sign on to the Internet and go looking for your future career at the big college across the state. After five minutes, the bell rings for the next period.

This 16 year old will not find any pulp and paper school with the resources at hand. They will either (a) choose another career and be forced to move away from home, or (b) give up on the idea of college all together. Sixteen year olds make these kinds of decisions about as fast as you choose a brand of laundry detergent at the supermarket. We cannot assume they are getting good, solid counseling and guidance. We cannot assume that their resolve to sticking to a plan is well developed yet. We have to put the opportunity directly in front of them and nurture them along. Edison was considered daffy and so was Einstein. It was only with maturity that they were accepted as brilliant, and it may only be with maturity that our future students develop a strong sense of determination.

Now, I am really going to step on some toes. The popular wave of changing the names of our pulp and paper schools to bio- or nano-something is not helping my theoretical 16 year old above. They know there is a *pulp* mill down the road and that is the key word in their educational search.

If you are involved in a university's pulp and paper school, try this test. Go to a neighbor or friend who does not have a detailed idea of what you do. Ask them to sit at a computer and find your college or department on your university's website. If they find it, see if they can further find a link to the scholarship opportunities uniquely available in your department. Don't help them, unless at least a half hour has passed.

I can only image what a bureaucratic nightmare it is to get something changed on a university website. However, alums have the power to make these things happen. Enlist them to put pressure on the university to at least give your pulp and paper school, and its unique scholarship opportunities, a chance to be found by an earnest, bright high school student. And show your own determination-- stick with it until the task is accomplished.

For safety this week, consider eye strain in the office environment. All of our Internet activities these days, coupled with lighting designed for offices pre-personal computer, puts our eyes at a real disadvantage in a subtle way we do not notice. Consider rearranging your office to fix the problem. We will talk next week. ##

Purchasing Follies

Week of 26 Jun 06

A longtime friend, a sales person, was recently relating his frustrations with a certain paper mill.

Apparently, through government mandate, this mill needs to solve a certain technical problem. My friend's company has the proven solution. The mill, however, has chosen a different solution, one which, in my friend's experience and professional judgment, is too expensive and will not work.

Nevertheless, my friend's company has quoted to the mill's request and is significantly higher in price than competitors when quoting this way. The mill has shut out my friend's company from even coming in to explain matters and offer their expertise with the brush off—you're too high.

This is not the first time this situation has happened. Specifiers become enamored with a particular solution, not with specifying that suppliers solve a problem with the best (technical and economical) solution. We have been subconsciously trained to do this in our own personal purchasing decisions. Automobiles come to mind as a good example of this.

Let's look at the difference, though, in this process. First, in purchasing our personal example, an automobile, we have no fiduciary responsibility except to ourselves and our family. Second, the car companies have lots full of cars, and their marketing, advertising, and sales job is to persuade you to buy a car they have already made. They flash a shiny solution to transportation issues in front of you and say, "You NEED this solution!" And you buy.

In our working world, however, things should be much different. First off, we have an absolutely solid fiduciary responsibility to spend the money the owners of our company have entrusted to us as wisely as possible. Secondly, most of the capital equipment we buy is not already made, so we do not have to buy "the ones on the lot," so to speak. These conditions demand that we specify solving our problem, not specify a particular solution. In my recent book, "The Lazy Project Engineer's Path to Excellence," on Page 29, I point out the differences in improper and proper specifications:

"However, avoid if at all possible actually sizing the equipment—hold the suppliers responsible for that. We will use a pump as an example of the wrong and right way to specify process equipment.

"Wrong way: 300 gpm centrifugal pump delivering 300 Ft Head at 1750 rpm.

"Right way: This pump will be installed on the second floor of the pulp mill. Conditions there are normally 95% relative humidity and 70 F in winter and 95 F in summer. Allowable floor loading is 400 PSF. The pump will be required to pump low consistency pulp of the specification (attached) supplied by the pulp mill from a point 10 feet below the centerline of the intake to a point 40 feet above the centerline of the intake. Total length of suction pipe is 45 feet and it contains 3 long radius elbows, one control valve (Cv to be supplied by valve supplier) two gate valves and is 6" 304L SS. The discharge pipe's total length is 110 feet and it contains 7 long radius elbows and is 4" 304L SS. Please specify motor horsepower and coupler size. Guarantee the pump for 3 years MTBF.

"See the difference? In the right way, you have asked the supplier to use their expertise (which is no doubt greater than yours because they deal with pumps every day) to properly size the pump. It is a performance specification. In the first case, you have taken on responsibility which someone else will gladly assume and do a better job of than you will."

I consoled my friend by observing that in a few years, after wasting capital funds on the wrong expenditure, and endless operating funds trying to make an incorrect solution work, that, if the mill is still in business, he may have the opportunity to specify and sell the correct solution.
And "if the mill is still in business" is not an idle comment on my part. I have been through many shut down mills and seen many mistakes that cost these mills precious capital and operating dollars and no doubt contributed to their demise. Wasting or incorrectly spending capital puts your job and those of your co-workers in jeopardy.

For safety this week, need I say buy your PPE (Personal Protective Equipment) from reputable sources with sound testing credentials? Using the wrong or inferior equipment to protect employees is inexcusable.

Be safe and we will talk next week. ##

Protecting the incompetent

Week of 2 Apr 07

This past month, I encountered yet another case of protecting the clearly incompetent employee. I suggested to the employee with which I was discussing a performance issue that a certain other employee be fired. The response was, "We don't want to see anyone lose their job."

How lame! The incompetent employee not only fails at their own job, they spread a standard of poor performance to everyone else. They are like an infection, crippling the whole organism, or a worm, devouring the whole apple. They must be removed.

One thing the private equity buyers in our industry are doing is finding these incompetent people and removing them. For instance, I received a call a while back from a retiree at a mill that had been bought out. He was surprised that the new owners had let a certain person go who had worked there for 35 years. I wanted to point out that "Mr. X" had only worked for one year and then did nothing for next 34 years. For once, I thought better of it and kept my mouth shut.

Every mill has these people. A mill is lucky to have only have three or four—I have seen places with 20 or 30. And such incompetence amounts to real money. Not only is the job that is supposed to be accomplished not being done, the mill is paying for it. This can easily be $500,000 to $1 million per year. All the while, the mill is trying all sorts of exotic and risky ways to make money.

I am not saying that getting rid of the incompetent is easy. Often, we have been walking by them for so long, we don't even know they are incompetent or that they are doing nothing. It takes a fresh set of eyes to see who they are. And then it takes a serious manager to remove them in a humane way. But they must go and go quickly.

One of the challenges to removing such people is that they have probably been doing the same tasks for a long time. Suddenly removing them will cause others to wonder, "Why now?" As a manager, you will have to ignore this and just move on. You can't let the incompetent stay just because you cannot answer this question. They are costing the site money every day.

One of the tricks used by mills with an incompetent person is to move them to safety. Big mistake. Your safety director should be highly competent. They have a big job to do and it needs to be done with the highest level of competence possible.

Be safe and we will talk next week. ##

Do they think we are stupid?

Week of 14 Apr 08

For some reason, a number of communications missives I have seen recently have agglomerated into this week's topic.

There is a billboard near my home, out on the main highway, that says: "Everything you need to sell your house: $595!" Well, if I wanted to sell my house, the only thing I would need is a qualified and motivated buyer. Is that what they are going to drop on my doorstep for $595? I doubt it.

I really like the ads on television about selling gold. The underlying message is "holding cash is bad, give us your cash and we will give you gold." Wait a minute. If holding cash is so bad, why do they want to exchange their gold for my cash?

Recently, I attended a meeting where the keynote speaker was from our industry. This person was basically mocking the Internet and telling us how important print advertising is and how it is growing. I agree it may be growing. I also note that Google's stock hit a high last fall and has yet to recover. But whose stock would you have been better off holding for the last few years--printing and writing paper producers' or Google's? As you know I am a huge cheerleader for our industry, but let's be realistic.

No matter in what forum you are receiving a presentation--your mill's conference room, a fancy hotel conference center in a big city, your company's headquarters--it always pays to step back a minute from the presentation and survey the situation. All speakers are trying to get across a point, their point, and it may be masking the important issues of the day. Often the ability to get to the real issue is what separates executive level individuals from the rest of us huddled masses. While Joe the production manager is telling the yarn about an unscheduled outage, the serious executive gets back on the real issue by asking pointed questions about the root cause of failure and how it will be prevented in the future.

Take graphs and charts, for instance. I have mentioned this before, but it is worth repeating--you have never viewed a graph or chart that was not designed to make the presenter's point. In other words, all graphs and charts are suspect, for what may really be important (to you) is what is not presented. Don't think this is true? Think about the last time you prepared a graph or chart for a meeting. The first thing you did was decide what you wanted to tell and how you wanted to present it. Then and only then did you start to work on preparing it.

I once worked for a bright Ph.D. in a development center of a major pulp and paper company. He had a great rule. If you were presenting a series of graphs on the same subject (say, experimental results with several trials), you were required to use the same scale from graph to graph for the abscissa and ordinate, respectively. It was startling how you could pick out dramatic differences in results when viewed this way. MBA types need to learn the same lesson. I've sat through many a presentation on subjects such as the flow of pulp and paper around the world. The presenters almost always select x and y scales that dramatize their point of view on each individual graph, thus obfuscating any comparisons between them. It is disingenuous to the audience.

So, don't get sucked in by presenters and their subtle

ways. And when you are presenting, do the best possible job of delivering the honest truth. In these ways we can advance our business.

Let us hope your management wants straight talk on safety statistics. Some twist and turn these to meet corporate goals. This is a travesty--they are playing with human life here.

Be safe and we will talk next week. ##

Where are your raw materials and where are your costs?

Week of 18 Aug 08

The pundits of 1910, despite the Schlieffen Plan, despite the arms race in dreadnought class warship construction, concluded that a war in Europe was almost impossible. Why? It was believed that important interlinking trade treaties (plus the fact that most of the royal leaders of the major European countries were cousins), made such a possibility unthinkable. There was just too much to lose in commerce and trade for anyone to think of paying the high price of a war for any reason.

Well, as we now know, one bullet through the body of one individual, wearing a funny feathered fedora, whose driver had made a wrong turn and was on the wrong street, and, actually would not have even been in that town had he (the victim) followed the advice of his trusted advisors, obliterated all the pundits' "wisdom." Not only was all the conventional wisdom of the day figuratively and literally blown up, most world events, nearly everywhere in the ensuing 94 years, can be linked to that bullet. The heck with interlinking commercial treaties.

In the past 10 years, particularly in the United States and primarily due to tax incentives (or disincentives, depending on your viewpoint), the pulp and paper industry has wholesale shed its most important asset: trees. On a worldwide basis, our industry has developed the mindset that we can purchase all of our raw materials and energy sources from those that know best how to manage them, run these materials through mills of nearly identical technology (in any given grade) and make indistinguishable products at a respectable profit. What foolishness!

In fact, this foolishness is further reinforced when one examines the cost components of delivering a non-unique product to an end use customer. If my back-of-the-envelope scribblings are anywhere close to being correct, the cost of that product controlled by the actual processes (including the energy consumed by those processes) within a paper mill are less than 20% of the final selling price. In other words, a 5% improvement in the cost of all things papermakers control (not counting the cost of purchased raw materials) can only affect the end selling price (or profit margin, if one can sustain the selling price) by 1%. What foolishness indeed!

In order to be competitive, one has to have a competitive feature. This seems like a simple idea, but apparently it is lost on many in the executive ranks of our industry. To repeat, you must have something with which to compete, some unique feature in raw materials, energy, additives, manufacturing, product features, or distribution. Everyone cannot do everything the same way and expect to earn extraordinary profit margins. The greatest visible example of an industry where the majority of players follow this strategy to their own detriment is the airline industry. This is an industry where your competitive advantage today is that you hand out (lend) free pillows and blankets to your customers!

The reality, in fact, is that if everyone in the same grade does everything the same way, not only can they not earn extraordinary profit margins, they cannot even earn acceptable profit margins. Players in an industry must have unique features, whether they be on the cost side or the customer feature side, in order to succeed for the long term.

It seems to me that the quickest and most economical way to become unique is in the customer feature area, adopting the ideas of the tissue manufacturers. Particularly in the printing and writing grades (and especially photo paper and standalone printer paper) there appears to be an opportunity to take one's message directly to the end user. Yet, no one seems the least bit interested in doing this, despite the 50 years of success tissue manufacturers have experienced following this path.

I have the belief, however, that some company will do exactly this and set the industry on its ear. For this is what happened in tissue--an interloper came to the market and made a uniquely feature product with distinguishable (to the consumer) claims. It can happen again.

In the meantime, find some way to make your raw material acquisition, production process or product unique. A little advantage can go a long way. It could be your "If only..." answer that I spoke of last week.

And keep your safety program unique, too. An always fresh safety program is one that works.

Be safe and we will talk next week. ##

You have got to be kidding!

Week of 14 Feb 11

I have recently found myself in a position, where on behalf of a couple of clients, I am soliciting information and bids from suppliers. Now, when I am trying to sell something, I am used to being treated rudely, my calls not returned and so forth. However, when I may be in the position to influence a major buy decision, you would think people might treat me a little differently...

Wrong.

The only conclusion I can come to from my most recent experiences is that most of you suppliers must have more business than you can possibly handle. There is simply no other reason why you would treat potential customers so rudely.

Here are a few examples I ran into dealing with large and small suppliers. These examples are all less than a month old.

1. After struggling to find a contact number on a large international supplier's website, I finally found it, buried on a back page. Upon calling it, I am connected not to a live, friendly operator, but to a computerized voice system. Listening to the selections available, the one for potential customers was about fourth or fifth down the list, right after the one where, if you were an employee of this august firm, you would press to get health insurance forms!!!!

2. In another case, I was accosted by a live operator who gave me "twenty questions" before she would allow me through to the party to which I wished to talk. It was only when I said that I might be placing a very large order with their company if I could only talk to the person who writes proposals did she relent and put me through.

3. In another case, a friendly, live operator told me she would put me through, but that I should not be surprised if my call was dropped, which happened all the time, in which case I would need to call back. Did she think or was she instructed to take my name and number and follow-up just to make sure my needs were answered? Of course not.

4. In another case, I asked a relatively small supplier, the owner of the company, to meet me at a mill site. He faithfully promised he would be at the appointed place at the appointed time. Was this promise kept? Of course not—he sent his flunky to see me, with no apology.

Were I competing against any of these companies, I could steal their business in less than a year. One would not need superior products or services. One would not need low prices. Just treat the prospects and customers like living, breathing human beings and I am sure in each case they would flock to me and throw off these sorry characters.

I have often said that selling is like courting, at least from the male point of view. If you want to win over their hearts and minds, you give them attention and heap boatloads of interest on them. Playing hard to get is for fools and the introverted.

I challenge all of you to look at your customer connection procedures. Have your friends call your companies and see if they find a friendly path to your door. Heck, hire me to do it—and you can reach me at 404-822-3412 or jthompson@taii.com any time I am not asleep.

For safety this week, I hope it is abundantly clear in your facility how one reaches emergency assistance. Test the connections quarterly at least—someone's life may depend on it.

Be safe and we will talk next week. ##

Jesse Jackson, Jr. and the AF&PA

Week of 25 Apr 11

For you readers outside North America, the name Jesse Jackson may hold little significance. However, the Rev. Jesse Jackson has long been a force in the African-American equality movement(s) here. His son, Jesse Jackson, Jr., is now a member of the United State Congress.

On Friday, 15 April 2011, Jesse Jackson, Jr., on the floor of the United States Congress said this, in reference to Apple's iPad device:

"...[the iPad is] probably responsible for eliminating thousands of American jobs." Explaining further, he offered, "Why do you need to go to Borders anymore? Why do you need to go to Barnes and Noble? Just buy an iPad and download your book, download your newspaper, download your magazine." Borders, a large bookseller in the US, recently filed for bankruptcy. Barnes and Noble is another large bookseller here.

Mr. Jackson's revelations about the demise of the printed word continued, but I'll not bother to bore you with all that. We in the pulp and paper industry have known about the demise of the printed word for nearly two decades. You long term readers know I have told you to get over it and move on to paper used for its tangible qualities (packaging and tissue).

Mr. Jackson's points are not the points I want to make, though. My question is this--where in the world is the AF&PA (the American Forest & Paper Association) and what have they been doing? They are, for all intents and purposes, the organization that (at least I thought until now) was supposed to keep the US Congress informed about the issues of the Pulp and Paper Industry in the United States.

It appears they have not been doing their job or I don't understand what their job is (I suspect it is the former). If I were the CEO of a large pulp and paper company, after the speech by the Honorable Congressman Jackson, I would have called the AF&PA and asked them how on earth a Congress member could display such a lack of understanding about what has been going on in the pulp and paper industry for the last 20 years? And if I could not get a satisfactory answer, I would ask for 20 years of dues to be returned to my company.

If the AF&PA has not educated every congressional member and staff persons on the conditions of the US pulp and paper industry and the loss of tens of thousands of high paying jobs, your humble writer is at a loss as to their purpose. If Mr. Jackson thinks the loss of the clerical jobs at the bookstores are something to become agitated about, image how incensed he should be about the high pay papermaking jobs and the small towns closed mills used to support.

As you know, I am a bit of a maverick in our industry and I cannot just stand by while a perfectly good industry goes down the drain. I could list a number of non-profit organizations (not the pulp and paper schools--the schools, by and large do a good job) which have failed in their duty to show at least a tiny bit of support to their members. And, again, I am no luddite, I firmly do not believe in propping up obsolete industries. However, I do believe in doing a great, creative job of redeploying our assets (people, trees, plant and equipment) as much as possible. Have you seen any conferences, talks, sessions or anything come out of the traditional organizations to deal with these matter? I haven't either, which gives you a good clue as to why I invest the time and resources I do in Paperitalo Publications.

I apologize for being a little upset myself this week, but I am sick and tired of seeing smiley faces instead of serious initiatives to address the issues our industry faces today. In fact, the ones I see addressing today's and tomorrow's issues are mavericks like myself working outside the conventional, "polite society" of pulp and paper's conventional coteries. Thank goodness for mavericks.

For safety, being a maverick is probably not a good idea. Plan your work, especially your non-routine work, and execute it carefully.

Be safe and we will talk next week. ##

Fun Facts to Know & Tell....

May 2004

I was sitting in a hotel room the other night ruminating over a few issues and started "googling" the Internet for some statistics. Technically, I was truly importing the data, for I was sitting in a hotel on River Road on the Canadian side of Niagara Falls and linking to the Internet with my wireless modem which was grabbing a signal from the United States, a half mile away. Although the sources are not cited here, rest assured these all came from legitimate sites such as the US Department of Labor, US Census Bureau and so forth.

In April, employment in the United States reached 137,691,000 out of a total population of 293,233,292 (46.95%) and another 4,598,000 were classified as "wanting a job." Doesn't that make the unemployment rate 1.56%? The US must certainly be the home of the idle rich if over half of us do not work and do not want to do so. Of course, these numbers include children, which mostly do not work in the US, even though in other countries children may be employed to make US children's shoes (see more on shoes below).

In 2002, the US drank about 3.4 billion gallons of bottled water. This is about 1.5 times the total beer consumption in Germany, but the startling issue is that the US imported 11.4% of this water (roughly 390 water towers full or

4,500 short tons per day). Have our labor rates gotten so high we cannot afford to manufacture our own bottled water?

The US consumes about 25 pounds of rice per capita per year, 4 pounds of which is consumed in the form of beer. The US imports a nominal $6.9 billion worth of paper and paper products (narrowly defined, does not include newsprint, pulp and so forth) per year as compared to $15 billion worth of shoes. On the $15 billion in shoes, we pay $1.63 billion in import tariffs. We pay $1.60 billion in import tariffs on automobiles, but we imported $110 billion worth of cars in 2002. From a tariff point of view, it appears more economical to ride than walk.

Currently, the US is exporting approximately $200 million worth of pulp and paper machinery per month. By comparison, the US is also exporting about $278 million worth of televisions, VCRs and so forth (not including stereos) per month.

The point? Anytime, anywhere you read statistics, keep in mind the author is telling you what they want you to know. Statistical data is like icebergs—the part you see is only a small portion of the whole. Beware the manipulation to make a point which all authors citing statistics (including me) employs.

When it comes to safety—do not become a statistic. Hearing loss is one of the most pervasive and insidious safety statistics around. It comes on slowly and imperceptibly. Make sure you wear your hearing protection all the time. Your children will thank you when they come to visit you in the old folks' home and don't have to shout. We will talk next week. ##

Forget work, it is the holiday season...

December 2004

The wife and I went to New York for the weekend. We like to do so in early December as it helps us get in the mood for Christmas (helps me get in the mood, she was there about July). Stayed at the Millennium Hilton, across the street from "Ground Zero," now firmly back in New Yorker's minds as The World Trade Center. Looking down on that site is still a somber view, however, like forests after a fire, signs of life are coming back—a new building is under construction on Vesey Street, the PATH train station with service to New Jersey is reopened and so forth.

We had dinner Friday night at L'Ecole, the French cooking school. It is the best bargain in Manhattan, prix fixe at about $30.00. Something like getting your haircut at the barber training school, but really no risk of bad results. It is on Broadway a couple of blocks north of Canal. Make reservations a couple of weeks in advance—the secret is out on this fine establishment (five or six years ago you could make reservations the same day).

Saturday, we first went to the Cloisters, another attempt by the Rockefeller family to bring culture to America. This collection of middle ages European religious artifacts is quite interesting. Stunningly, some of the lower chambers reminded me of old paper machine basements (the ones with brick arches supporting the machine track, for instance.

The Cooper Hewitt museum is worth visiting only because it is located in Andrew Carnegie's old home. I immediately saw the resemblance between this house and the chain of libraries he franchised after his death. Suspect they used the same plans to save on architects' fees.
There is a fantastic exhibit of Gilbert Stuart portraits currently on exhibit at the Metropolitan Museum of Art. Most US schoolchildren are familiar with Mr. Stuart's work from the print of the unfinished portrait of George Washington that is in many schools. Mr. Stuart did finish many other portraits of our Founding Father, and the Met has managed to collect them all in one room. ##

Potpourri

May 2005

I bought an alarm clock a few weeks ago for a trip I was taking. I wanted something simple and reliable. I bought a "Baby Ben." If you were alive in the 1960s in the United States, you or your parents no doubt had one of these. It winds up, has one alarm setting and is still cute, even today. Only discernible differences are three: (1) the case is now injection molded instead of a steel stamping, (2) it is now made in China instead of Illinois and (3) it has a sticker indicating you are not to throw it in the trash. I digress. The beauty is I can wind and set it faster than I can even think about which alarm to set on my dual alarm clock radio and I actually burn a fraction of a calorie doing the winding. Lesson: all technology "improvements" are not.

Innovation is alive and well in our industry in corners of our industry, though. I visited Tim Campbell at Jackson Paper, in Sylva, North Carolina a week ago this past Tuesday. This is the kind of scrappy, hungry company we need in our industry. Jackson Paper is working on a chicken litter bedding made of single faced corrugated. The beauty of this is that in the manufacture of the paper to make this single face, they can add chemicals and medicines that help keep chicken house disease and odor under control. Tim is quite modest about this product--it is still in early testing--but what a breakthrough innovation! By the way, this mill, for years, has been one of only two known mills in the US that operates a skiver-- a piece of equipment that butt splices two rolls of linerboard together to make a wider roll. Paper machine width is not a limitation for the innovators in the mountains of western North Carolina.

We certainly need creativity, a subject I have been writing about here and elsewhere. The problem as I see it is that organized creativity is stifling. It takes small groups, doing tasks with small budgets, but driven by a need to survive and a strong desire to succeed, to make innovation work. Organized innovation and creativity, alas, appear to be an oxymoron.

You might be a slovenly bureaucrat if--you eat better on company trips, on the company's money, than you do when spending your own.

For safety this week, be alert for fatigue, your own and that of your colleagues. Many a person tries to be a hero on an extended shutdown by working ridiculously long hours, with no particular purpose. Stop this activity in its tracks. We will talk next week. ##

Travel Season in the Northern Hemisphere...

June 2005

Here in the Northern Hemisphere, personal holidays are in full swing (for some reason we call them vacations in the U.S., the rest of you call them holidays). I thought this might be an opportunity to go over a few tricks of travel I have learned over the years.

First, I like to stay with one chain of hotels, a chain that has segmented itself into several classes of properties, low, mid and higher priced. This way, I can get frequent traveler points accumulated from every stay. They add up. Several years ago, my family spent a week in Hawaii at a very nice resort on these points. This summer, we are using them in Rome. Sometimes, since I am in business for myself, I use them on sales trips charged to my company.

There are some hotel chains that should be avoided like the plague. They may have fancy commercials on television, but basically, they buy worn out properties from other chains and invest little in them. You probably know who they are.

Room selection. If I am traveling from one town to another on business and staying in places without dramatic views

(Meridian, Mississippi and Decatur, Alabama come to mind), I ask for a room on the first floor. A properly functioning elevator will cost you at least 5 minutes at each end of your day. An improperly functioning elevator can be a disaster. Avoid elevators unless you have some burning desire to be above the first floor. Another matter about elevators, try to avoid rooms near them on any floor unless you are soothed to sleep by them swishing by day and night.

Also, of course, avoid being near or over bars and so forth. One time, years ago, I was staying at a famous hotel that papermakers like to use in Appleton, Wisconsin. I was over the bar. Finally, about 2 a.m. the bar closed. At 3 a.m., the carpet installers arrived to rip out and replace the carpet. I was, shall we say, grumpy the next morning. Be aware that atrium hotels sometimes have suicide jumpers. I stayed in an atrium hotel in Houston about 20 years ago for two nights and there was a jumper both nights (different people, of course). One of them landed in front of express checkout. I checked out the normal way and went home--somehow the glamour had left traveling.

Food is a problem for me on the road. I hate to go to a restaurant and eat by myself (I enjoy nice restaurants with plenty of company). Consequently, I eat way too much fast food and delivered pizza. If anyone has any ideas on how to eat healthy when traveling alone, I am all ears.

Long trips to other countries. Pack light, pack light, pack light. Also, avoid taking expensive jewelry and other valuable personal items. The chance of loss or theft is too great to risk Grandpa's retirement watch.

You might be a slovenly bureaucrat if--you use an assistant or subordinate to make your travel arrangements (I am talking about business travel arrangements, I already assume you are not audacious enough to use an assistant for personal arrangements). With today's Web-based ability to make travel arrangements, you can easily do in 10 minutes what it will take you and an assistant half a day to do with a travel agency. It is all about quick choice review and decision-making. Using the Web and doing your own puts the decisions right in front of you and eliminates the endless back and forth options and choice discussions.

For safety this week, we will stick to the travel theme. Carry your passport, money and credit cards in a place where a thief will not normally look. We will talk next week. ##

Dress sizes, scales, lawyers, seat belt signs, politeness and the degradation of society

July 2005

Policies and trends in the seemingly unrelated lists of items above are causing civilized society great harm. These trends and policies are institutionalizing and normalizing white lies and the acceptance of standards of performance less than the very best. Let me explain.

It has been widely reported that dress sizes are no longer

accurate, especially in the high-end shops. Being male, I have never understood the mystery of women's dress sizes anyway, but apparently the more you pay, the larger a, let us pick one, size 5 is. The manufacturers are lying to the customers to make them feel better--make them feel that they are smaller than they really are.

Next example: I was on a cruise ship recently. Since I weighed myself the day before I went on the cruise and the day after I got off the ship (thankfully, those land based scales--and I used exactly the same one at both end--showed no gains) I can absolutely prove the ones in the fitness center on the ship were set five pounds light. Why would they do this? To make the passengers feel good in a gluttony of food, of course. Same logic as the dress size gambit.

To get to the cruise ship, I flew on an airplane for nominally 10 hours each way. On the embarkation trip, the pilot definitely erred towards leaving the seat belts sign on if there was even a hint of a bump in the next 1,000 miles. Why? My thinking is that he wanted to make sure there was no chance a passenger in the aisles would be slightly jolted and sue his company. The flight was so long and the signs on for such a long portion of it, that people ignored them to go to the bathrooms. But the airline was protected if anything happened, for those passengers up and about were clearly violating a warning from the airline.

Then comes politeness. We often "damn with faint praise" our coworkers who do not quite live up to the standards our organization requires. We let them continue with our full blessing despite an undisguised half attempt at doing their jobs. It is easier to let them go on rather than risk the consequences of confrontation. This slowly degrades our enterprise.

So to my point--the more we accept, throughout society, things that are not quite truthful, not fully honest, the more our society deteriorates because we transfer these little snippets of life to life as a whole. Excellence is abandoned. Honesty is difficult to find, causing one to lose their bearings. Life becomes a walk through carnival mirrors, with true reflections hard to discern. Truth and honest feedback, absolute necessities in striving for excellence, are impossible to find and we individually and collectively lose our grip, causing a slow slide to mediocrity and the loss of principles we hold dear.

You might be a slovenly bureaucrat if--you do not seek out additional assignments actively. It was reported last week that AOL (America on Line, a division of Time Warner) recently surveyed office workers and found they admitted to goofing off two hours per day on average. Those surveyed said they do not have enough to do. Suggestion: email me if you do not have enough to do--I can definitely think of some things you can do to help the organization that employs you. ##

The mailbag is bursting...

August 2005

The readers of this column have been vocal about a number of issues recently. We will start with a general comment regarding the "Dark Side" column of a couple of weeks ago. Paraphrasing, many of you wrote saying that I must have been a fly on the wall of your organization because the column fit perfectly. One even said I absolutely must have been in a certain department at a certain large corporation in 1969. Not so. It was discouraging, however, to see so many relating to and identifying with such conditions--this is an indication of what trouble we are in as an industry. However, as a sampling of what I received on this subject we will use this one:

*"Holy cow, Batman! Do you realize how closely your "Dark Side" attributes for individuals come to describing the **corporate** characteristics of at least two of the largest pulp and paper companies in the US?"*

Regarding whatever happened to buggy whip manufacturers and whether they had the insight to move to emerging technologies (the readership of this column can supply answers to anything):

"In reply to your reference to buggy whip manufacturers, I worked for Eastman Kodak in their paper mill (electrical/ mechanical plant engineer). In the 1880s a prominent Rochester [New York] resident was Mr. Frank Strong, a renowned buggy whip manufacturer. He helped George

Eastman by financing Eastman Dry Plate & Chemical Co. George gave Frank 50% of the profits. That went well for both of them!!!"

More details on the background of Nokia:
"Nokia actually started up with a paper mill before moving to rubber, then cables, then telecom ..."

"I have indeed seen Nokia tires in Finland."

And, finally, regarding scooter rentals in Messina, Sicily, a response from England:

"The mistake the guy made in Messina was using GOOGLE. Had he used Dogpile, as I have just done, he would have found at least five suitable rental agencies in Messina.

"Try it. Select "advanced search" then enter the specific words motorcycle rental messina and see what you get.

"Better luck next year.

P.S. hope I am not a slovenly bureaucrat for sending this in Company time!!"

This brings us to the most popular department ever in the history of this column. You might be a slovenly bureaucrat if--you use blank taxi receipts to inflate your expense report to cover your personal expenses while on a company trip. (I know you are Shocked! Shocked! to think anyone would do this.)

For safety this week, I would like to draw your attention to the initiative called ICE. ICE stands for "In Case of Emergency" There is an effort under way to promote cell phone owners to place in their cell phone directory the word "ICE" and for the number, put in the number of the person you want called in case of an emergency. This way if you are found unconscious, emergency workers can scroll through your phone directory to ICE and call them. Sounds like a good idea.

Be safe and we will talk next week. ##

The "Costs" of Progress

Week of 13 Mar 06

Back in my first job (mid 1970s), we could see computers coming, but were not sure what form they would take. We, of course, had no idea that there would be personal computers on everyone's desk, but were already, on a limited basis, using time share terminals to do complex calculations and so forth. Our vision in the engineering department of a major consumer products company, however, was naïve—we thought with the advent of all the computer power coming around the curve we would have all sorts of time to "do our jobs right."

About 15 years ago, I attended a conference where one of the learned speakers told us how unconsolidated the paper industry was and how the industry would become healthy once consolidation took place. Once again, we in attendance all applauded and looked forward to that day.

Now, rumors are afloat of possible further mergers in the uncoated free sheet business here in the United States. Such rumors include ideas like Weyerhaeuser buying either Domtar or Boise.

Friday night a week ago, we were out with a couple, the husband of which works for Domtar. He was concerned that Domtar may soon close their satellite technical support office and have them work from home. I say, in light of these recent rumors, he may have a bigger concern than that—he may be, what we call in polite professional society, "redundant."

All of these vignettes I have just recited are related. These matters (except for the last) have all come to pass and all have left our industry with fewer employees, both salaried and hourly.

Those of you who have read my writings for some years know that I applaud a healthy industry, even when that health comes at the cost of having fewer jobs. In reality, we can do nothing about it, for improved competitiveness and higher standards of living for society as a whole always mean doing more with less.

The learning to come from this is that as employees we are all competitors and those of us with the most flexible attitudes, the most valuable skills, and the healthiest mental outlooks are going to survive. The rest of us are going by the wayside. The only personal successful path in the future is one of being current and ever prepared for change and flexibility. Long term careers in our industry will be built on this in the future.

Whatever you do, be safe and we will talk next week. ##

Ridiculing Paranoia

Week of 8 May 06

I hesitate to start down the path of this week's title, for some may view this as merely confirmation that old Jim has lost it. However, I plunge forth with my usual fearlessness.

The reader must admit that often when someone brings up the specter of an impending event, the reaction is often one of ridiculing the messenger. This also often happens when one in the know is describing the actions or cultures in an organization.

Spoken or unspoken, the reactions are something like this, depending on the circumstances:

1. That will never happen
2. Impossible
3. They don't really behave like that, do they?

The truth is, there is often more truth in what we perceive as paranoia than not. I have observed this in many places and many circumstances.

It is particularly evident when a place of employment is going to shut down. As an outsider, all the signs are there, but for the employees, facing the truth is more than they can handle at the moment. It is like the reaction when one receives bad news from the doctor.

Groups of people—a company, a department, or so forth—may act in a way that seems bizarre when compared to the norm. Yet, it is sometimes true (look at some of the CEOs that have been in court in recent times). But most of us deny the conditions until confronted with them in bold black and white.

We are also guilty of perceptions that, while not exactly in the areas discussed above, can be expensive to us. For instance, this past winter I was talking to a supplier about providing certain consulting services to them. For a while, they were interested, and then the interest fell off—normal. A couple of months later, I actually wanted a budget quote from this supplier for a project I was working on with a mill. I left a voice mail message, no response. I sent an email, no response, except after about two weeks, my email message, according to my email provider, was deleted without reading. This supplier lost out on the early activities of a potential USD 10MM order. All because of a perception they had formed.

It is difficult to just process all the data we receive daily. It is even more difficult to review all the data we receive each day objectively. However, those that experience business and personal success often have found a way to do this. I think they are also very aware of their own subconscious data and bias filtering and work hard to keep it under control.

Spend some quiet time thinking about what you don't think about—the automatic perceptions and biases you employ each day. They just may be costing you time and money, in fact, I am almost certain they are.

Paranoia does not exist in safety considerations. You cannot be too paranoid about your actions and those of the people and things around you.

Be safe and we will talk next week. ##

What's in a Graph?

Week of 19 Jun 06

Sitting in a meeting the other day, it was interesting to watch a presentation of graphical information. The presenter had several large graphs, perhaps a half dozen or more, and was intent on making an implied point with them.

This got me to thinking about graphs in general. There have been a number of books written on this subject and we'll mention a famous author in the field before this column is over.

When you are presented with graphical information, my watchword is caution. You are probably being set up; for it is almost guaranteed that the information being delivered by the presenter is done in such a fashion as to make a point of the presenter's choosing. How do we know this? Consider the situation with the tables turned: unless you are preparing graphical data for your own personal use, you are preparing it in a way to make a point to your audience. Every other presenter is doing the same thing. Hence the recipient must be cautious in order to sort through the presentation and draw their own conclusions.

There are a few overt clues which can lead one to an appreciation for the deceptions promulgated by the presenter. The first clue is the selection of the scales for the abscissa and the ordinate. The abscissa, or x-axis, is often a time line. Ask yourself why the presenter chose the particular time line attributes (start, finish and scale). They had a reason and the sooner you figure out the reason, the sooner you will understand the real point they are trying to make (not necessarily the one they say they are making). Likewise with the ordinate, or y- axis' scale, starting point, and stopping point all say something and most likely that something is being subconsciously transmitted by the presenter.

Then there is the relationship between the abscissa and ordinate. The selection of these scales' relationship to each other as relates to the data plotted drastically affects the slope of graphical lines or the "noise" of wildly gyrating data point collections. Again, the presenter chose these to make a point, a point they may not overtly verbalize.

Rookie or unsophisticated presenters leave clues to their objectives all over the place. The biggest mistake they make in failing to hide their intentions is to use different scales as well as different starting and ending points from graph to graph in a related collection. Such presentations are blatant attempts to distort the matter at hand. An honest presenter attempting to show data from graph to graph but needing more detail will show the same abscissa and ordinate scale from graph to graph and then show a complimentary enlarged graph if more detail is needed.

Again, the caution is to watch out for graphs – they seldom present facts in an unbiased fashion. For more on graphical techniques, I recommend the books of Edward R. Tufte. This author is an expert on presentation of data and offers especially clever examples of how to present a multitude of data in two dimensional views.

For safety this week, be watchful of the presentation of safety data. There is probably no other field of common data in pulp and paper mills more blatantly manipulated than this.

Be safe and we will talk next week. ##

Two little noted, momentous anniversaries

Week of 10 Jul 06

This past April, and then just last month, there were two anniversaries that I dare say have touched nearly everyone on earth, although at first blush they seem quite provincial in nature. They both have had a huge impact on the pulp and paper industry.

We will take the second one first. This was the passage, 50 years ago, June 1956, of the federal highway act establishing the US Interstate Highway System. This was the cornerstone legislation of President Eisenhower's first term. This single bill kicked off a cultural and industrial revolution which has not yet run its course. Over the next 25 years, more than 40,000 miles of express style highways were built in the United States.

General Eisenhower's vision and motives came from two places. The second of those was his observation of the German Autobahn, built just prior to World War II. The first was his own career problems at the end of World War I. At the end of World War I, Eisenhower was a young officer in the US Army. His job, for which he was promised a promotion when completed, was to redeploy the materiél coming back from Europe to various forts and posts in the United States. The road system here was so poor that this took many months more than originally anticipated, thus delaying his promotion.

In April 1956, 60 days before the passage of the law, 50 trailer trucks full of goods, without their tractors, were loaded into an old tanker in New York harbor. They were sailed to Houston, where they were unloaded, hooked to other tractors, and taken to their local destinations. This was the precursor of the now worldwide ubiquitous shipping container.

How have these events affected us all? In immeasurable ways. The shipping container obsolesced the existing ports and stevedore system. For instance, New York harbor went away and shipping moved to New Jersey (where there was plenty of flat land for cranes and shipping container lots). Likewise in London—the Canary Wharf redevelopment is a direct outcome of the obsolescence of stevedore-staffed ports.

The US Interstate Highway System symbiotically mated with the shipping container. This is no more evident today than if one travels Interstate 16 from the port of Savannah, Georgia to I-75 and then on to Atlanta. This is shipping container alley, as trucks with one or two shipping containers bring goods into the hungry mouth of Atlanta.

The interstate system further drove car purchases and this grew economies worldwide. The shipping container became the physical internet, easily moving goods intermodally without costly transfers. This all has not been without a price, though. The interstates led to the homogenization of the United States, where now, if one is dropped blindfolded into suburbia, it is likely they will be hard pressed to tell exactly where they are—all look nearly the same. The US thirst for oil is no doubt driven by the interstates. On the other hand, excellent quality inexpensive goods are now available to more people on earth than ever before, thanks to the humble shipping container.

But I want to end on another note. I have been thinking about this and trying to find a way to convey it to you, especially you many readers not in the United States, without sounding like an arrogant American. Last spring (2005), as some of you know, I set out on an extraordinary personal journey, planned over many years. In seven days, by myself, driving my 2005 Honda CR-V, I drove the 48 contiguous US States. This was a journey of a little over 8,000 miles, or an average of nearly 1,200 miles per day. It was done with the utmost concern for safety (I slept in a motel room every night) and would have been impossible without the Interstate Highway System. Yet, there was one other key element that is a clue to a source of strength of the US economy. It is this: over the entire journey, despite the fact that the license plate on my car was in its home jurisdiction for only the first hour of the whole week, I was never stopped once by any authority and asked what I was doing, where I was going, or just to "see my papers." To the contrary, I finally started approaching police officers and having them sign my witness book, which they all did graciously and with best wishes to me. To my knowledge, there is no place else on earth (except perhaps Australia) where one could make a trip of this length and not be stopped several times. This freedom of movement is a vital component of economic strength.

These are key elements for economic growth and represent an opportunity to bring the same benefits to all humankind. This opportunity is still in its infancy.

For safety this week, I have never been in a pulp or paper mill where there was not a tremendous amount of inbound and outbound traffic (unless it was shut down). Be safe around this traffic, and, if your assignments take you near or you are in charge of loading or unloading, be extra careful, please. We will talk next week. ##

World War III and the pulp and paper industry

Week of 24 Jul 06

As of this writing, the conflagrations in the Middle East and the problems in North Korea are being labeled WW III by some pundits. I am not sure if this is what history will call it or not, but it serves our purposes here.

I wrote a few weeks ago about running our businesses lean and mean and protecting the supply chain contents with insurance. I stand behind that as a normal course of business, but suggest that if a few ships are sunk, or if there is even the threat of sinking ships due to hostile actions, all bets are off and most likely all insurance policies are cancelled. It is this latter scenario we will discuss this week.

The supply chain around the world works nearly seamlessly these days. It is so seamless, in fact, that we often forget that much of it occurs in international waters or airspace. In the case of serious hostilities, we will quickly learn what it means to try to conduct business outside of each of our countries' sovereign borders. If history is any guide, it will not be a pretty sight.

Conventional wisdom in 1914 was that Europe would not go to war, for interlocking trade treaties and interdependent commerce would prevent it. Ironically, the beginning of World War I coincides almost exactly with the first ship (the SS Ancon, 15 Aug 1914) to pass through the Panama Canal (see below). WW I proved that mutual defense treaties trumped international commerce.

All we need is a serious hint of disruption of international trade, and you can throw the current rule book on supply and demand out the window. Every domestic supplier in every affected country will suddenly find a ripe market for their products as imports are disrupted. At the same time, their dependency on imports of their own for raw materials and energy will not be sated. Those with domestic supplies of inputs will prosper, those serving primarily as tolling facilities will flounder.

One thing we do not realize is how precarious the choke points, particularly in international shipping, may be. The Suez Canal is probably the most obviously precarious one for transshipment of goods. It is almost within visual sight of hostilities and was closed for many years after the wars in the 1960s. The Straits of Hormuz are a well-known choke point for 25% of the international oil traffic.

The Panama Canal is also an interesting dynamic. Humankind has now succeeded in building ships that fit within inches of the locks on all sides, but still require some off-loading/reloading at each end because of weight (the ships are less buoyant in the fresh water of the Canal and the landslides into the Culebra Cut continue to this day, limiting ship draft). So, the ships are partially off-loaded and this cargo transported the length of the Canal on a railroad owned by a company from the eastern hemisphere. It is 7,872 miles further by ship from San Francisco to New York if the Canal is not available.

What is the prudent pulp and paper company to do? Lock up supply of raw materials from domestic sources, even if you have to lock them up at much higher prices in contracts that are enforced only under certain conditions. For if international trade is disrupted, expect prices for goods to soar. Under such conditions, one would be able to afford more expensive raw materials and still make great margins— look at the oil companies, their raw material goes through the roof and they book historically high profits—not bad work if you can get it.

Now, a disclaimer, in order to keep myself out of trouble with the anti-trust people: what I have just suggested above is merely an idea in a hypothetical case. I am not suggesting, purporting or promoting that anyone go out in a joint or collusive fashion and lock up supplies of anything. We are talking hypothetically here, and we do not endorse anyone behaving in a manner even suggestive of anti-trust behavior under any law or spirit of the law anywhere.

I do believe we should, however, share everything we know about safety. We can never learn too much when it comes to saving our fellow workers from injury or even death in the workplace.

Be safe and we will talk next week. ##

What Research & Development can we share?

Week of 25 Sep 06

This topic was discussed at a seminar I attended last year. I came away not completely happy with the answers promulgated.

Last Thursday, I was sitting on the banks of the Wisconsin River with a good friend discussing the same topic (OK, we were in a restaurant, but it was on the banks of the Wisconsin River). He was talking about and expressing frustration over the idea of learning more and more about less and less—refining one's research to the point that it may never have a useful application. I have thought about that since then and may have the inkling of some answers for him and for the rest of us.

First, I recommend that one recall Nip Impressions® of a couple of weeks ago, where I was talking about professional explorers (and our lack of need for many of them in our industry). Refining that further, I think we can distinguish between research on natural objects (such as the human body) and synthetic objects (such as paper).

Researchers on natural objects are explorers. In fact, if one researches living tissue of any kind or, in the earth sciences, geological formations, one is doing that to understand illness, genetics, longevity or natural phenomenon. I have never heard anyone say, for instance, that their research on a living animal was for the purpose of reorganizing its parts, e.g., "I think the head ought to be where the toes are." Granted, we sometimes mix up genes and make hybrids, in both plants and animals, but, in general, drastic redesign is not the objective. One can be a researcher with exploration as their goal forever on natural objects.

It is different with synthetic products. Since synthetic products, by their very nature, are made by humankind, it appears in most cases perfection has not been achieved. Thus research can be constant and always seeking a better solution than we had in the past. This is not exploration—it is creativity. In fact, one way to look at competitive conditions is to say, if no other competitor is available, "Let's compete against what we made today." In other words, we can always make synthetic products better by applying creativity. The personal computer is an excellent example of following this line of research. If computer manufacturers had not competed against their own products, Mr. Babbage's work would be state of the art.

If we think of paper, it is an agglomeration of a group of somewhat dissimilar materials—cellulose, chemicals, starches, clays, pigments and so forth. I don't think association of this collection of materials has been perfected and, more importantly, probably never will be. There is always a way to assimilate these things together and create a new class of materials—hence this could possibly be the focus of collaborative basic research: "How many ways, for instance, can we make cellulose and clay stick together and what are their uses?" This is a fundamental pre-competitive question.

There is a profession that perhaps we can follow to find the ways to be creative about these agglomerations. It is, and no joke intended, the profession of stand-up comedians. These people make us laugh by linking dissimilar things or events in improbable ways. They are very creative. This is exactly what we need to do to make new competitive and useful paper grades.

For instance, I got to thinking about baked Alaska, paper, dry ice, flash heating, sintering and powdered metallurgy. I put these things together in the following way. One thing we can do very well in this industry is make boxes of elaborate configuration, cheaply. Let's say, then, we make a paperboard and spray it with layers of powdered metal. Then we make this special paperboard into a box of a configuration we want. As an aside, we make a block of dry ice that will fit exactly in the paperboard box. We put the dry ice in the box, and we put the whole thing in a flash furnace, which will rapidly heat the paperboard box with the powdered metal coating to a very high temperature. The box burns, the coating sinters, and we have a metal box of very peculiar properties. We melt and recover the dry ice which served as a form during the flash heating (it behaved as the ice cream does in a baked Alaska during the flash heating). We have a finely formed metal box. You will admit this is an idea agglomerating the improbable. And, we can also see that it would take much work in the laboratory to make the ideas of this paragraph into a commercial product.

And this is but one example of what we need to do to make new and better products from our old reliable material, cellulose. Creativity is the path we must follow, not exploration.

Remember, hot and cold things can both be safety issues. Watch your behavior around both of them this week. ##

Fear

Week of 9 Oct 06

I have been told I have been caught only once writing a column that is repetitive in nearly five years of NI. I am proud of that record, and hope in the future I can continue with fresh material until they pry my cold dead hands from the keyboard.

In a larger sense, though, I write about only a small collection of topics centered around professionalism, integrity, trust and competency. Granted, there a many permutations on the way to ignoring one's fiduciary duty (my loose, collective term for the previous), but in general, you will find me in this realm as an overarching theme.

My subset this week is fear. Most are afraid of many things. A friend of mine's favorite terminology for most of these fears is "jousting at windmills," an activity in which the famous Don Quixote reveled.

However, it is funny how our fears cause us to make poor decisions at work, both in a fiduciary sense and in a personal career sense. I am going to list some of the fears I have seen paralyze people:

1. Fear of incompetence or being found incompetent

2. Fear of staying at a certain company

3. Fear of going to a new company

4. Fear of promotion

5. Fear of stagnation

6. Fear of moving children in school

7. Fear of moving to the South

8. Fear of moving to the North (note: you have to live in the United States to understand 7 & 8)

9. Fear of taking an international assignment

10. Fear of new co-workers

11. Fear of reorganization

12. Fear of retirement

13. Fear of not being able to retire

14. Fear of a new boss

This list can go on forever and ever. Isn't it interesting how many of the items on this list are paired with those diametrically opposed?

The point I want to make again, however, is that our fears, mostly imagined, often cause us to make poor decisions. How to make good decisions? Sit down and write down your fear. Keep writing until you get to the root cause of your fear. For if you do this with diligence, you will find your fear may really be trivial. And when you find your fear to be trivial, you can make a decision based on facts.

In my own case, I have several fears. An example is a fear of heights. When I was a child, I was afraid to stand at the top of the open stairs in my grandfather's house. I have worked on this to the point that I have been to the top of continuous digesters (but I still have not gone to the top of the Eiffel Tower). I have had a fear of leading a dull and boring life, and I have beat that one (but it has been the cause, no doubt, of some bad decisions along the way).

The point is recognize and dissect your fears. You cannot make good decisions until you do so.

Regarding safety, you have no doubt been trained to observe the conditions around a prostrate unconscious person before approaching them. Whatever you do, though, please make sure you do not use that training as a fear excuse to avoid helping another human being in distress.

Be safe and we will talk next week. ##

Inaction

Week of 16 Oct 06

Long ago, in a micro economics class in college, I remember a statement from the Samuelson textbook that went something like this: "For all the caution and unwillingness to take risks in business, it is surprising how innovative and vibrant the business economy is." I put this in quotes, but it certainly is not an exact quote, given I read it approximately 35 years ago and how selective my memory can be at times. However, it will suffice here as it seems to be more accurate than ever.

It appears to me, and admittedly this is from anecdotal perceptions only, that employees in businesses have become more, not less, risk adverse in the ensuing three decades. This has not necessarily served individual businesses well, for too much caution has caused more than one business directly in our industry or in ancillary businesses to fail.

This couples to my theme of "fear" from last week. Modern inaction seems to have roots in several soils. The first is that of analysis. Professional business people of today are taught many techniques of analyses in their advanced education experience. Some become quite fond of using these for the sake of using them. They produce reams (perhaps I should say megabytes) of formulae that they believe means something but in reality never provide a valuable answer.

The second soil is that of our current operating climate, particularly here in the United States. The collection of laws known as Sarbanes-Oxley appears to have instilled in some executives the fear of doing anything which might be construed as aggressive. In their abject terror, they have commanded from on high that the minions not do anything aggressive, either. Now, if you work in a company that has adopted this posture, you may not recognize the connection between Sarbanes-Oxley and this new behavior, for it is couched in phraseology that does not link it to same (not that anyone is trying to hide the link, they are just using different words they think necessary to justify and rationalize their pronouncements to the huddled masses in the trenches). Sarbanes-Oxley, by the way, is a minor contributor to the private equity movement— companies privately held are not subject to most of its onerous reporting requirements, which may be as high as 4% of revenues for companies less than $100 million in annual sales.

The third soil is that of control. Since the introduction, a decade or so ago, of massive software programs whose intent is to control and report the most minute details of the largest enterprise, managers have been emasculated. It as if HAL, of the movie "2001, a Space Odyssey," has taken over. Middle management is beholden to the rules and reporting structures of the software and dare not disobey it.

What to do? To keep with my allegorical leanings this week: adopt hydroponics. Hydroponics is the science of growing plants in water, without soil. In other words, find sources of nourishment for your business that are not location bound. Look at your competition, your customers, other industries, anywhere to see what is working for others and what trends seem to be telling you. Transform your business daily. You can do this as an individual, a division, a small company or a mega corporation. Get active before rigor mortis sets in.

And by now, you know what I am going to say about safety: safety is an active state of mind, not an inactive one.

Be safe and we will talk next week. ##

Product Variety and Differentiation

Week of 1 Jan 07

Television was an infrequent visitor to our home when I was a child. Dad thought it quite idiotic that anyone would sit in front of a box and watch it. He caved in twice and bought sets. As each one wore out, they were a long time being replaced.

I do remember, however, 50 years ago happened to be a time when we had a television set. For on New Year's Day, 1957, the H. J. Heinz Company of Pittsburgh, Pennsylvania declared it "their year" for they were (and are) the company that claims "57 varieties." Their commercials ran on television several times that day.

Heinz figured out early on that one could expand their business by expanding their product offerings.

In the 50 years since I saw that commercial, there have been many attempts at product differentiation, some successful, some not quite so great.

Some of the direct-to-consumer marketers have done the best with this effort.

However, I want to spend some time today talking about basic paper manufacturing's efforts.

We are not so good at product differentiation, although it seems like there would be many opportunities, if we approached it carefully (I have known some who have not and have seen their "grades" balloon to unmanageable numbers). The key to me is closer cooperation and communication between sales and production. For the higher margin of custom grades is giving the customer something really of value to them (meaning we can make higher margins) while not tweaking our standard product much at all.

I know one little mill, for instance, that will hand ream cut orders as small as 500 pounds. The customer pays a very high price for this, but in this case, there are several very loyal customers that want this service. It would not be worthwhile in a big mill, but it is a nice little profit addition for this one.

It seems like there ought to be a number of opportunities in the brown board business to add a service of high value. This might be, for instance, an automatic return of trim from sheet plants for recycling at the linerboard mill.

Perhaps this could be done as a "credit" so that the cost of linerboard that becomes trim never hits the books at the sheet plant.

Our mills tend to want to make the same thing every day. That's desirable from a production point of view, but may not mean the highest margins for the mill. Seriously explore your business for hidden margins in 2007.

Today, your 2007 safety record is perfect. What are you going to do to keep it that way?

Be safe and we will talk next week. ##

Consumer Reports for Industry

Week of 19 Feb 07

Here in the United States we have an organization called Consumers Union that publishes a magazine called "Consumer Reports." This organization, and its reporting arm, the magazine, accept no advertising. They are clean.

If you are not familiar with this organization, they test all sorts of consumer devices from small to large. They report on and rank fairly the products they test. Their existence is quite a boon to consumers.

We need such an organization in the pulp and paper industry. Fair and balanced data across machines doing the same task is nearly impossible to find.

What are the barriers to such a system? Cost, of course, is one. A second may be legal ramifications—our industry does not have a stellar record on anti-trust. A third may be where to house this organization.

Once one overcomes the first two (and I think they can both be overcome) the logical domicile for such activity is the Institute of Paper Science and Technology or one of our other fine institutions. Our fine scientists at such places may not see this as their role, but I see this as an expansion of their role. Additionally, and without a doubt, new research projects will spin out of these routine examinations.

So, to review, a category of machines or instruments are brought to a non-biased institution for examination and certification. Three of eight pass. The data is shared with the institutions' members and anyone else who signed up for the study: all manufacturers share in the results. The deficient manufacturers are offered help to correct their equipment.

I think this is all straightforward. Have I missed anything?

Thank goodness safety equipment is tested again and again. That, however, does not relieve you from the details of a "common sense" check every time you are around such equipment.

Be safe and we will talk next week. ##

A bit of nostalgia

Week of 5 Mar 07

After last week's harsh dose of reality I thought I would delve into a fond old memory that has long been obsolesced by the Internet: the local cigar, newspaper and magazine store. We had one of these in the small town where I grew up, in fact, every small town had one.

The aromas were divine! The smells of pipe tobacco, cigars, and hard candy all mixed together and topped off with the oiled wood floors. It astounded me that one could go in a local shop and find The New York Times, the Chicago Tribune and other such papers. This was, indeed, a window on the world, no less fascinating than sitting around our short wave receiver in the evening to find out what we could hear.

And there was another little benefit of this store. When, as children, we needed boxes for science fair projects, we just stopped by the store after school to pick up cigar boxes, which they saved just for us. Such a nice box was so handy and the price was right—free.

We have many nostalgic matters, even in our own mills. I remember working for a mill manager who answered the phone, "_____ 's wire." It wasn't a phone to him—it was a wire. This is not so long ago—he has two sons quite active in the industry. I can even remember doing budgets with a pencil and nine-column accountant's green paper. I have not seen a pad of that in years. Of course, a

Marchant rotary calculator (which weighed about 30 pounds) went along with this exercise.

Fortunately or unfortunately, depending on your point of view, these matters are all behind us. The race belongs to the swift and accurate. I see it as part of my job here each week to persuade, cajole and inspire you. We can dip into the nostalgia once in a while, but then I need to say, "I know it was nice, but we live in a different world now."

One way you can become involved in the past while working in today's world is to become actively involved in one of the many museums of papermaking. One of these is the Robert C. Williams Paper Museum at IPST, along with the George W. Mead Paper Education Center right next door. In the Fox River Valley, there is the Paper Discovery Center and the Paper Industry International Hall of Fame. There are also many others, for instance, RittenhouseTown. I hope to assemble an online directory of North American paper related museums one of these days, so if you want to write me in order to point out a great museum that I missed, I would appreciate such correspondence.

Sometimes we have to work around antiquated machines—and you know what I will say next: that's no excuse for poor safety habits or records.

Be safe and we will talk next week. ##

How I spent my Winter Vacation

Week of 21 May 07

First, we hope you enjoy our new look. Many of you have asked for a website for Nip Impressions and now we have one. You will now be able to review each week's Nip Impressions in its entirety by going to www.nipimpressions.com and clicking on "Newsletter Archives." You will also be able to search old issues for a particular term with the "Search" function. We will start building an archive with this week's column. We have worked diligently to try to make this as smooth and glitch-free as possible. If you notice anything we can improve, please let me know via an email to one of my email addresses.

Now, off topic this week. In late October 2006, I developed an abscessed tooth. My dentist hustled me off to the root canal specialist (everyone is a specialist) and we thought we dispatched this handily. In a follow-up visit the next week, however, the root canal specialist was not happy (because the abscess had not receded) and sent me to an oral surgeon to see if the abscess could be relieved. However, instead of relieving the abscess, by the next morning, the oral surgeon took biopsies and hustled them off to my favorite cancer doctors at Emory University here in Atlanta (I had non-Hodgkin's lymphoma 7 years ago and was declared "clean" of that one long ago).

Result? I had Burkitt's lymphoma, a disease that has now been tentatively linked to farm kids from the days when we shoveled fertilizer and pesticides without protection. It has also preliminarily been linked to teenagers that handled tobacco plants which brushed against their bare arms. Farm wells may also have been contaminated from some of these sources. Guilty on all counts. I won't bore you with the 10 extended stays that I had at Emory University Hospital, multiple blood transfusions, and the countless outpatient clinic visits (starting in mid-November and ending this month), only to say that my prognosis is excellent at this time (a PET Scan on 10 May 07 could find no cancerous cells in my body). There are a few points worth making, however:

1. The outpouring of support I have received from friends in our industry around the world has been humbling. We are truly one big family. Thank you—it would be impossible to thank all of you personally—except to say a special thank you to my wife, Laura, who took me on as a full time job for the last six months as she put her own career on hold to make sure I was extremely well taken care of. Her countless drives through Atlanta traffic from our home to Emory and back were a perilous enough hardship in their own right without even mentioning the nights she spent in my room on the "comfortable" overnight chairs (my new slogan—if you want to be clean or get a good night's sleep, don't let yourself be admitted to a hospital).

2. You need to know cancers are divided into two major categories: soft tissue and tumors. Blood cancers (leukemias, lymphomas and certain other cancers) are soft tissue and treated in an entirely different way than

125

tumors. Tumors may often involve surgery and chemotherapy as well as radiation; soft tissue types usually involve chemotherapy and sometimes include radiation.

3. If you have something funky happening with your body, get it checked out. Now. This week. Early detection is your best friend.

4. I have seen a number of new patients at Emory and even had an acquaintance diagnosed with lymphoma this winter. For all new cancer patients, their biggest enemies are denial and delay.

5. Despite excellent diagnosis, one person I know has chosen to order an elixir over the Internet that is supposed to be a cure all for everything. Do you think all the research and insurance dollars being spent on treatment would occur if it was this easy? Such actions are just a form of denial.

6. Go to the best cancer center in your region, or if that is not good enough, the best one anywhere for the kind of cancer you have. This is easy to research these days. You do not have a cold. It is unlikely that you are going to get the best treatment possible for any cancer, just to pick on a mill town, if you happen to live in Quinnesec, Michigan (don't write me about my random choice, please!). Travel, sometimes long distance travel, is often necessary.

7. I am struck by the progress, at least in my field of current interest—lymphoma, that has been made in the

last seven years. It is phenomenal, and from what I hear, is proceeding apace in most other areas of cancer research.

Conclusion—many cancers are no longer a death sentence, as long as the patient is not in denial and wastes valuable positive early action.

Consider for your next safety meeting inviting someone in from your local cancer society chapter for a broad overview on what are the symptoms for various cancers and how one should go about watching for them. Anecdotal evidence suggests that for every hundred employees you have one or two in denial right now—and cancer does not care what their job title or age may be.

Be safe and we will talk next week. ##

Global Shrinking

Week of 22 Oct 07

We have covered some ground-breaking subjects here in the past. You may recall a few years ago when we discussed the flier that was in my water bill that admonished us to not allow leaves to fall in creeks in autumn. Well, we've fixed that one here in Georgia—we are in such a drought that there are no creeks. The symbiotic relationship between mother nature's drought and humankind's urban sprawl sucking up what water we have, thus averting the pollution problem with leaves and water, would bring a tear to one's eye if we were not so parched. Reminds me of General Jack D. Ripper (in the movie Dr. Strangelove) who said, "We must guard against the depletion of our precious bodily fluids."

You may also recall when we covered PETS—the People for the Ethical Treatment of Steel, whose mission it is to eliminate arc welding and the trauma that may be caused by the heat in that process as the crystalline structure transforms from martensitic to austenitic and back (they prefer bolted fasteners at PETS).

Such columns come so infrequently because we must make sure we have our facts straight ensuring we live up to our self-imposed mandate to give you only the fully researched truth, no matter how inconvenient it is for our research staff (we are not sure that is a requirement for winning the Nobel Peace Prize, but it is our standard here at Nip Impressions). We have done our homework, as you will see from the bibliography at the end of this column, and you are reading it here first—the news is so fresh that I have not seen it anywhere else. It is only through diligent research and determined investigation by my aides, especially Fred, that I have been able to assemble the shocking truth.

Friends, we are suffering a crisis of monstrous proportions: Global Shrinking. It has been irrefutably caused by humankind. The good news is that there are some tiny signs that it is starting to be reversed.

This may seem counter-intuitive, for one often associates warming (the news in the popular press) with expansion. We are prepared to give evidence contrary to this here and now. Apparently this crisis we have so recently discovered started about two hundred years ago and has grown exponentially since that time.

As just mentioned, a couple of hundred years ago, the primary means of transportation was horses. As an aside, according to a study done by the state of New Jersey in the early 1990s, the mean production of horse manure per day is 51 lbs. per 1,000 pounds of live weight. This was determined by, and I am not making this up, "grab samples"[1]. By the way, according to the same study, this is the lowest "exhaust" per 1,000 pounds of live weight amongst a number of animals: dairy cattle, beef cattle, swine, laying chickens and broiler chickens (it would just wear one out trying to catch those grab samples from chickens, wouldn't it?).

Further, if one looks up the statistics on the Pony Express[2], one finds they averaged about 10 mph and the horses were changed every 10 miles. Thus, assuming a day's rest and a 1,500 pound horse, the horse "exhaust" was about 7.65 lbs per mile. Comparing this to the automobile's discharge of roughly one pound of carbon dioxide per mile, one might think there has been a great improvement, particularly since the grab samples indicate (I'll skip to the summary) only about 3.9 streptococcus colonies per mile in the horse exhaust[1]. Ah, for the good old days when the transportation system did not emit carbon dioxide! There were other downsides, though— around 1900, in New York City, there were apparently about 15,000 dead horses[3] continuously in the streets—it wasn't all wine and roses.

Yes, humankind invented the tools of global shrinking in roughly this order: newspaper, railroads, telegraph, automobile, radio, UPS[4], airplane, television, FedEx, fax machine and internet (although it may actually have started—we don't have the proof yet—when curlers discovered that brooms make the stones go faster). All of these apparent "improvements" must take their share of the blame for global shrinking, even if the streptococcus colonies have been reduced. In fact, we may be suffering from a shortage of streptococcus colonies (there are rumors they may be placed on the Endangered Species List). Yes, we must hang our heads in shame (until we can firmly put the blame on curlers) that our industry started the headlong rush, the now shorter rush (due to Global Shrinking), to the abyss with newsprint.

The extent of the problem was driven home to me recently as I read a biography of Albert Einstein (by Walter Isaacson)[5]. On page 310, it is noted that Einstein was warned by Svante Arrhenius, the Chairman of the Nobel Prize for Physics Committee, that he (Einstein) should postpone a trip to Japan starting in October 1922, because "It will probably be desirable for you to come to Stockholm in December" which would be impossible in those days before serious global shrinking (if he were already in Japan at the time). It should be noted that Einstein went to Japan anyway, being the modest man that he was. But to the point—the globe must have been much larger then, for there is no other explanation for his not being able to get to Stockholm in a short length of time.

And this supports our thesis, for what has changed since that time? The Earth, inclusive through the Ionosphere, still contains essentially the same amount of each element as it did then. Sure, we have flung a few scraps of aluminum and titanium to the moon and beyond, but these are insignificant amounts in the larger picture. We have cleverly rearranged some elements and molecules into other elements and molecules. Additionally, we have taken a few molecules from beneath the Earth's surface and thrown them into the atmosphere, but the conservation of matter still prevails. We can definitively say nothing has arrived, nothing has left the Earth in the last few centuries. Global Shrinking is the only possible explanation for Einstein's travel dilemma of the 1920s.

Attempts to stop global shrinking actually started some time ago, but were not recognized as such. In the late 1960s, early 1970s while Britain and France jointly the developed their SST (Super Sonic Transport) ultimately manifested in the Concorde[6], the US shut down a similar project on March 24, 1971[7], an act that serendipitously slowed Global Shrinking. The British and French finally saw the light a few years ago (the last Concorde flight was November 26, 2003), abandoning the Concorde and thus making the Atlantic Ocean just a little larger for overseas travelers. It just shows that with determination, Global Shrinking can be curbed.

In another area, while there are hopes of some promise in reducing Global Shrinking, the results are mixed. I speak of the Amish[8]. Their settlements are spreading (a good thing), but they have taken to riding in automobiles as long as they are driven by us non-Amish (a bad thing) which makes the apparent distance between their settlements shorter. They have found a technicality around engines, too—diesels don't have spark plugs (hence no electricity—a no-no in their world) and they are using them with abandon, but not yet for transportation. One can drive through Amish country in the summertime and see hay bailers powered by diesel engines but pulled by horses (at 51 pounds of exhaust per animal per mile due to the slower speeds in the field and the heavier weight of draft animals). By the way, it takes four draft horses to pull a hay bailer—you do the math.

Never, fear, though, such matters have their ups and downs as we attempt to solve the crisis du jour—Global Shrinking. Just remember, you heard of Global Shrinking here first. So, do your part, walk, not ride, the next time you want to go to Disney World.

Now, I must ask that you not shrink or shirk your duties to yourself and your coworkers when it comes to safety. My goal is that you are safe and healthy, even if the Earth is reduced to the size of a ping pong ball (40mm)[9].

Be safe and we will talk next week.

Bibliography

[1]http://www.epa.gov/waterscience/guide/feedlots/tech orse.pdf

[2]http://www.ponyexpress.org/history.htm

[3]http://www.economics.ucr.edu/papers/papers03/03-10.pdf

[4]http://www.100ups.com/?WT.mc_id=123919

[5]Isaacson, Walter. "Einstein: His Life and Universe." Simon & Schuster, New York, 2007.

[6]http://www.concordesst.com/

[7]http://www.unrealaircraft.com/classics/sst.php

[8]http://www.blackwell-synergy.com/doi/abs/10.1111/j.1467-8306.1978.tb01194.x

[9]http://pingpongballs.net/ ##

Research Funding Fallacies

Week of 29 Oct 07

In the United States, Europe, Japan, Australia, New Zealand, and a few other places, we, the pulp and paper industry, have moved towards a model that funds research through primarily government-backed programs. We have come to this point through external pressures, false ideas and laziness. This model, although it should not necessarily go away, is not serving us as well as others could.

The external pressures come from stockholders and their proxies, stock analysts. This group demands accountability from our corporations (a good thing) but has no way of measuring anything but short term (read: the next 13 weeks') results. Hence, funding research, whose results are more likely to be measured in 13 years than 13 weeks, was largely cut from the budgets. Unfortunately, an industry, whether an individual company or a consortium of companies, that does not do research is planning for no future.

Some do believe in a future, so they have looked around and said, "Aha! We'll get the government to fund our research. It is a way to recoup not only our tax dollars but some from others—we'll get free research! Aren't we smart?"

These ideas can be ripped to shreds in a heartbeat. First, the pool of tax money obeys the law of conservation of matter, or, stated another way, it is a zero sum game. There are only two sources of tax money: (1) tax revenues and (2) our grandchildren (borrowing against the future). When you are at the top of the tax heap, as virtually every corporation is, you are not getting anyone else's tax money, you are just getting a portion of your own back. If you are further down the food chain, so to speak, it is different—you can pick up other's tax money for your constituents. In fact, there is a very senior senator from a mountainous eastern state here in the United States that has made a career of that. He brags that his state receives more from the Federal Government than it pays in in taxes—he is correct and his constituents apparently believe him for they have named virtually everything in his hometown (Beckley, West Virginia) that doesn't move after him.

Tax money for research comes with many strings and hidden costs. Using the US as an example, I'll point these out. First, we must lobby Congress to get it. Second, even with lobbying, it only comes through channels and for purposes defined by Congress, necessarily a political process that has little to do with succeeding in business. Third, it comes with a handling fee, for there are bureaucrats that must be paid salaries in order to determine who actually gets the allocations approved by Congress. Fourth, steps one through three take an inordinately long time. And, finally, there is loss of control: just like everywhere else, those who write the checks say what gets done by when.

However, these steps are not the most insidious part. In the modern system, it appears we have turned many researchers into funding lap dogs. It was not always this way. Coincidently, this month we are noting the launch of Sputnik fifty years ago in October 1957. I remember my dad reading about this in the newspaper, figuring out when it would come over our town, and dragging us out in the back yard to see it. Sputnik awakened the United States to the space race, resulting in the formation of NASA (National Aeronautics and Space Administration), and with the election of President Kennedy, a definite goal: to get to the moon by the end of 1969. The only way to do that was with government funding and, as we all know, the goal was reached, with the loss of only three lives—a remarkable safety record for such an audacious plan. NASA has floundered aimlessly ever since.

In many government funded research areas today, at least from my perspective, we have forced our researchers to kowtow and bend their innovative thoughts to fit some convenient funding scheme. In some cases, they have lost their integrity completely. I gave you an example of how that is done in this column last week, entitled "Global Shrinking." On one level, you were probably thinking I was poking fun at Mr. Gore, and I was just a little. But on a serious level, I was illustrating what a researcher that has lost their integrity may do or one that spends an inordinate amount of time filling out government funding applications may be forced to do (a researcher's time is a zero sum game, too). Some of you wrote commenting that I must have spent a great deal of time on that piece of drivel. I designed it to make it look that way—if I spent more than two hours on it, I'll eat my hat. Even the details about Einstein going to Japan and quoting exactly from page 310 in that biography was easy—that just happened to be where I was in the book—I spent no time researching it. The style, acknowledgement of research help (Fred is my dog), a bibliography and so forth, also made it look "researched" even if it was obviously a parody.

Unfortunately, I fear, we are in danger of getting what appears to be real research done about this sloppily. Material that has format but no substance. We are not necessarily protected by peer review, either. My personal experience in that endeavor is telling. I was asked to be on a peer review committee. I was vetted by an untrained administrative assistant. After three or four papers, I resigned, for I felt I was in over my head. The sobering thing is that I had to resign out of my own convictions; had I not done so I would probably still be on it today.

So, what must we do? First, we must recognize that good research is the path to the future. Second, we have to recognize that government funding, while appropriate in some cases (energy is probably one of them) is not a "one size fits all" answer to our research needs. Third, we have to stop being lazy and educate stockholders and analysts, showing them that it is in their best interests that we fund more research directly (and point out that it is subsidized by the government as a tax deduction). Fourth, we must responsibly place the funds with appropriate organizations. Fifth, we have to manage the research, which we get to do if we write the checks. And finally, we must get outsized, practical results for our stockholders for our investment. It is not easy, but it is a better path.

You would not think of cutting off funds for safety training and safety devices. Make sure safety is at the top of your funding list.

Be safe and we will talk next week. ##

Contracts

Week of 17 Dec 07

You engage in contracts every day without thinking about it. "I'll be happy to bring you a cup of coffee" is a contract.

Lawyers particularly like this type—it is verbal and can generate large fees if one is passionate. Remember the poor dry cleaner that lost the guy's pair of pants and was sued for millions?

Verbal contracts should be avoided, or, at the very minimum, one must recognize that they should not engage in a verbal contract that can cause them a loss greater than they can happily absorb, either through liability exposure or loss of expectations. People engage in so-called "verbal agreements" either through machismo, laziness, or ignorance. If you think many verbal agreements do not end in failure look at the US divorce rate: 50% of these "verbal agreements" are broken. A whole class of lawyers makes their living from these failed verbal contracts.

A famous failed "handshake contract" was initiated in 1939 by Harry Ferguson of Ireland and Henry Ford. This involved building Ford tractors with the "Ferguson System" of implement connection (essentially what is known in agriculture as the "three-point" hitch). In 1952, Henry Ford II and old Harry Ferguson settled their arguments for the unheard of sum of $9,250,000 (about $70 million today) to Mr. Ferguson plus lawyers' fees of about $3 million ($23 million today) for each side. So much for verbal contracts. By the way, Ferguson took the money, bought into the Massey-Harris company and changed its name to Massey Ferguson (part of AGCO today).

In a mill, particularly in the heat of battle, it is easy to forgo contracts. Often there are several contractors on site continuously. If something goes bump in the night, one of these is called out to handle extra or specialized duties. No contract is written. These situations are dangerous if there is not some over-arching agreement, for a liability can be incurred by either side that carries unspecified damages. The proper way to avoid this is to have a blanket agreement with such contractors that covers any time they work on site. Your purchasing department and legal staff can help work these out and enforce them. If you do not know for certain that such documents exist, you might want to stroll down to the purchasing department and check out the matter.

Sometimes today, we are prone to "over-contract" matters. This is due to the tremendous growth in tort claims and government regulation. You may, like me, enjoy reading what I call the "lawyer labels" on consumer products. All of them are there for a reason, including such apparently silly ones as "don't use this hairdryer in the shower" or "the lawnmower should be kept on the ground while operating." These became written contracts because some consumer sued over the manufacturer's failure to preclude these uses of the product.

The most important concept I want to leave you with on this subject is the idea that you engage in many contracts every day, you just often do not give them any thought. The point at which you should go from verbal contracts to written is when your exposure has the potential to become more than you are comfortable losing. At that point, get it in writing.

Safety is a contract, too. Our employers are obligated to provide a safe working environment with safety equipment concomitant to the application. As an employee, we are obligated allow ourselves to be properly trained and to follow the training. Failure here can be much more than mere money.

Be safe and we will talk next week. ##

Caution: You are entering the perception zone

Week of 28 Jan 08

Most of my adult life, I have heard the phrase, "Perception is reality." This is often a cautionary warning as to how others might perceive what one is doing, or how they look and so forth. I want to talk today about when perception is not reality and how this might affect our actions.

As my contemporaries and I have gotten older, I have noticed a peculiar set of attitudes: we have become our parents. We often think the younger generations are daft, don't know what they are doing and so forth. More interestingly, we think we are the first to discover this. This is not so. Our parents felt exactly the same way about the younger generation when we were the younger generation. They wept for the future—how could they possibly leave the world in our incompetent hands? Of course, that was not their choice, time marches on, and responsibility left their hands, however unwillingly they relinquished it, and fell into ours, no matter how ill prepared we were for it. This process repeats itself again and again.

Yet, I find my contemporaries and myself marveling as if we have discovered something new—that it is a surprise that those younger than us are inexperienced or that the youth want to change the world now—traditions and protocol be damned. Have we forgotten in our youth when it was said, "Never trust anyone over 30?" Our parents must have alternately chuckled and shivered over that one. These are misperceptions caused by time and our place in it.

Physical location can cause misperceptions, too. We tend to view the world from where we live. Where we live is a tiny place on the globe of which few are aware, but we don't see it that way. Modern communications, especially television and the Internet are helping us gain a broader perspective, but we still have a tendency to see the world for our little vantage point. And this vantage point may be distorted or largely incorrect.

Business is another area where perception may not be reality. If you become too engrossed in a single facility or a single niche in the world of business, you may think the world revolves around that point. I once made a career move, going from an operation where two or three hundred people reported to me to an office of eight. I was shocked at how disorganized and mismanaged an office of eight could be. Both facilities thought they were key to the daily revolutions of the earth and the changing of the seasons. They were not, for today neither one of them any longer exists.

Most high profile people, either in business, politics or

entertainment that get into trouble arrive at such a position due to misperceptions about themselves or others around them. Just look at the notorious cases of the last few years. These people had other problems, but a big share of responsibility for their downfall was their perception of themselves and others.

The truth is, a vast majority of the world's population has never heard of the place you live nor knows what you do. You may live in a large and recognizable place, such as Manhattan or London or Beijing, but there is a level at some point in even these places where only Google Maps can find you. The rest of the world has not given you any thought.

So what is the point? Be careful of your own feelings of importance, for, unfortunately, they do not travel well over long distances, sometimes even over moderate distances. Also be careful of your views and awareness of the actions of others—they may be more important to you than you realize. In fact, the most startlingly are those you have not even considered existing who suddenly show up to change your life (such as a tax auditor who last week you did not know was even alive and is suddenly your most familiar acquaintance).

Finally, be aware that prejudice is a function of distance. My observation is the closer we are to someone else, the less prejudiced we become. Prejudice toward other people, regardless of the reason, can only be successfully carried out at a distance. I am sure if you and any other individual on the face of the earth found yourselves equally equipped and stranded on a deserted island, you would be best pals within a week.

When it comes to safety, perceptions play a key role. How many people, interviewed after an accident, start with, "I thought…" Such perceptions can be deadly.

Be safe and we will talk next week. ##

Fred & Balto

Week of 16 Jun 08

Last Thursday, about the time you were receiving last week's Nip Impressions, my dog Fred and I were living the pathos of a story much like the famous story of the sled dog delivery of diphtheria serum to Nome, Alaska in late January 1925 (well, maybe not that great, but it will serve the purpose here).

If you are not familiar with the serum run, it is the famous real life story for which the now annual sled dog race, the Iditarod, commemorates. I love dogs, and every time I read the story of the serum run, I cry. Dogs blew their lungs out and mushers (drivers) took extraordinary risks, crossing lakes they were not sure were frozen enough to carry them. One team averaged an astonishing nine miles an hour for 28 miles. Others had to deal with four foot drifts of snow. Balto, the last lead dog in the relay, ran twice as far as normal (53 miles in total), leading the team by scent—the musher said he could not see his glove in front of his face, the whiteout conditions were so bad. By the way, it was -53F at the time.

Anyway, last Thursday, late in the day, a client wanted a document from me with my real, signed signature on it. I prepared the document and a FedEx envelope and Fred (my dog) and I started out walking for the FedEx box, 7 blocks away (I could have driven, but I did not want to increase my carbon footprint). Would we make it in time?

The Georgia sun was blazing, it was over 90F. The first block was not too bad; I was in shorts, T-shirt and sandals, appropriately dressed for the weather. Fred picked at a few dried worms (his favorite road food) but I urged him on. Soon, Fred figured out we were in a hurry, and got down to business, pulling hard on the leash. Blocks two, three and four passed quickly. Five was a blur. At six we ran into a partially decayed dead squirrel, which Fred thought he had to stop and roll around in. I was now pulling the leash. Got Fred back in the game, and he took the lead again. We trotted across the parking lot, hoping the Fedex box would show the green sign. Victory! We had won the race in severe weather conditions. We dragged ourselves home—Fred's tongue nearly reaching the ground, me covered in sweat.

I have probably "Fedexed" a maximum of five documents this year. Ten years ago, the kind of work I do for this client would have necessitated daily trips to the FedEx box or the UPS box with ten pound packages—all paper. Then, Adobe Acrobat PDF (a registered trademark of Adobe Systems) became popular. Now, clients such as this prefer nearly all my work in the PDF format, delivered electronically. Not only has the PDF format eliminated a very large use of cut size copy paper, this change, along with the Internet, has eliminated two administrative assistants' jobs in my office (which illustrates there are sometimes hidden costs to paper usage). The down side for me is I can now produce clean revised copies in the format clients want while I am on vacation—and they know it.

Now, I don't mean to hammer on examples of loss of paper demand as it may seem I often do. I do intend to do so often enough that those of you in denial awaken to the point that you carefully analyze your grade's situation and take appropriate action before it is too late.

Take the above example, for instance. There is an opportunity here for a high value paper product that does not exist. For this client of mine came back the next day and wanted a notarized copy of the document Fred and I so "heroically" delivered. Why can't we make a paper and link with some sort of system on the Internet so that one could notarize a document without being present in front of a notary? Maybe this involves making a printer that has the security of the Pitney Bowes postage meter. I am sure law offices would buy such a machine and the special paper that goes with it. Maybe the paper turns pink when the proper safeguards have been met and it declares itself notarized. Maybe it actually has a section that self-embosses like a notary's seal. I don't know, I'll let you great product developers figure this out, but it looks like a high margin product that some paper company, probably in conjunction with a printer manufacturer, could make into a great business.

My overall point is some grades go away, but others are

developed that are higher margin, better businesses than the old. It is just a matter of using one's brain power and initiative to develop them. Nothing stands still and you can be successful for a long time to come if you realize this.

In this heat, if you are in the northern hemisphere, make sure you stay hydrated. A wash-up, down day, or emergency shutdown can create very hot working conditions. Keep yourself and those for which you are responsible safe and healthy as they work.

Be safe and we will talk next week. ##

Who cares?

Week of 4 Aug 08

This column is going to perhaps sound like, as we say here in the US, "sour grapes" but I think it has to be said.

When it comes to scholarly articles, we are all quite familiar with the tried and true cross examination method of "peer review." However, when it comes to plain old trade and association magazine articles, no such thing exists. In fact, there is no such thing as background checking for such articles, at least not any of which I am aware.

Here at Paperitalo Publications(TM) (a new name we are introducing to describe our family of publications: Nip Impressions, PaperMoney, Capital Arguments, and The Thompson Private Letter), at least we know where our information comes from and we strive very diligently to provide honest and verifiable material (Hey, my name is on this stuff). If it is from other sources, as much of PaperMoney is, we so indicate or it is so obvious that we do not have to do so. It is called journalistic integrity.

Yet, in some other industry publications, I often wonder what in the world is going on. Do these people think we are stupid? One hardly needs do any background work on some of these articles to know that, at the very least, more background work is needed. In other cases, where I don't think I am particularly knowledgeable of the circumstances, one finds stories and propositions that are remarkably, incredibly without credence. Such stories range from the "scientific" (needs to be in quotes unless the authors want their work judged against that of alchemists of old) to management where "great" touchy-feely managers are lauded while anyone with any kind of an ear to the ground knows people are running screaming from the building at the very enterprises they manage.

Now, in some areas, there are articles and reports on matters that can best be identified as experimental. And this conflicts me, for I believe we must experiment and try new things—long term readers know I believe this to be important. However, such matters are often not identified as such. Perhaps their sponsors are concerned that such identification would result in loss of funding or other support, I don't know. But it seems to be to be a bit disingenuous to present as fact something that we know is not—at least not yet. Don't get me wrong, I am cheering for such things to win, but when I go to a ballgame, I don't brag about my team winning the game until they do.

In the 1990s, I was heavily involved on Wall Street in the financing of recycling projects. Some I worked on as a proponent, on others I was asked to provide forensic consulting when they failed. One of the most interesting was when a bank asked me to go look at a project that had been built and was not running. When I came back to their offices, they asked me, "Well, did it look to you like they invested xx millions of dollars there?" I said, "Yes, indeed it does." The bankers smiled. Then I said, "But you have asked me the wrong question. The correct question is, 'What is it worth today?' to which the answer is scrap value." As you can imagine, they were not happy, even though it was mostly stainless steel.

Some of the schemes being floated and written about today may need to be done for the greater good of advancing our knowledge. However, it will not be long before the investment in them, I fear, will be nothing but scrap value.

So, who cares? I know the readership in our industry is smarter than some of the authors give them credit. So, when someone reads a sampling of these miracle or fantasy articles foisted on them as fact, they do the natural thing—become cynical. This cynicism is a contagion that then spreads throughout their place of work, one person at a time. Pretty soon, it spreads throughout the industry. And just beyond that phase, everyone starts making things up when the facts are not convenient. And then, we all go out of business, for our business becomes one based on fairy tales.

All I can say is, we are going to continue to tell the truth as we see it. I am going to try to find ways to do more background checking so you can continue to be assured that we are doing the best possible job in the industry of bringing you good data. In other words, we actually want to earn and keep your respect so that when you read something from us, you are confident you have the best information possible.

This, of course, runs a financial risk for us, for Paperitalo Publications depends on advertising revenues in order to survive and thrive. If advertisers think the frankness of our discussions here cause them problems, they won't be here. But when it comes to truth versus money, I don't have a problem—we'll stick to the truth. And, dear readers, if we miss the point or the truth occasionally (we are not perfect) we will continue to be open and transparent to your criticisms.

By the way, I operate to the same principles in our consulting business. Take for instance last week—we had a Request for Proposal for a specific project. After others and I had spent considerable time trying to see how we could respond, we declined. We concluded that a response, which we surely could have made and won (and made a nice profit doing), would have resulted in a conclusion worthless to the prospect.

To run a good safety program, you need the best information possible, too. Are you sure the safety data you gather from your departments is accurate and factual?

Special safety note: QUIT KILLING OUR WORKERS. As I was sitting looking at the computer this past Tuesday evening, here comes the sad news of three fatalities at PCA's Tomahawk, Wisconsin mill. Add to that the fatality at IP Vicksburg this past spring and it has been a very bad year indeed in the North American pulp and paper industry. Who is killing our workers? Probably an attitude of inattention to details on the part of many. The conditions we work under can be dangerous and we are all responsible for keeping our attitude correct and our attention high at all times.

Please—be safe and we will talk next week. ##

The Lunacy of Small Groups

Week of 15 Sep 08

When I was in the 6th grade, in the spring of 1962, at Kyle Elementary School in Troy, Ohio, our principal and mathematics teacher, Mr. Raymond P. Daniels, told us that it was impossible for humans to mentally visualize more than four objects at once. He told us to do the following thought experiment: visualize one owl on a branch, then two and so on. He said that we could easily visualize four, but when it came to five, our brains would group them as three, then a space, and two. This is one of the many pieces of trivia that has bounced around in my cranium for obviously a very long time. (Really useless information: our school, Kyle, was named for a union officer killed in the battle at Shiloh, Tennessee almost exactly 100 years before the Daniels' visualization).

When it comes to our work associations, we also operate in small groups. In fact, I don't care what your rank is in your organization, nor even how big your organization is, I'll bet you regularly interact with only six to ten people on a daily basis. It is outside your comfort zone to deal with any more than this habitually. In other words, at the executive office level or at the janitorial level, your coterie is small, familiar and contented. This is very dangerous, for it fosters a fortress mentality.

It has been observed, but not understood, that when ovulating-age human females are organized in a close knit group for a length of time (say a military brigade or an all girls' school), their menstrual cycles tend to move into synch with one another. To my knowledge, this phenomenon has still not been explained, although it has been verified many times. All snickering and giggling aside, I seriously see this as an interesting parallel to the situation which is the thesis of this column.

A great book that tangentially approaches this subject is "A Confederacy of Dunces" by John Kennedy Toole (sadly, published posthumously after Mr. Toole committed suicide). This beautiful work of fiction chronicles a group of what one might charitably call "eclectic" people in New Orleans in mid-20th century.

Small group lunacy occurs more often than we realize. This close coterie with which we associate each day gradually develops nearly identical outlooks, opinions, and responses. They begin to believe they hold the truth and others outside the group do not. Opinions from the outside world are observed and synchronously criticized without thinking. The phenomenon of "group think" takes over, resulting in reality and rational observation being placed in jeopardy.

The world saw a case of "group think" turned upside down recently when one of the US presidential candidates chose an unconventional running mate. I believe much of the uproar can be attributed to the choice being outside the conventional wisdom of those perceived to be "in the know" regardless of their own loyalties. In this case, the group engaged in "group think" was very large indeed, orders of magnitude larger than the size I am discussing here.

This has been much studied in places such as airplane cockpits, ship bridges, and other such critical groups, especially when the "group think" approach has led to tragedy. From casual observation, I think I can easily make the case it happens in companies, too. The results can be just as tragic, although most likely in a financial or employment sense. One could even argue without much of a stretch that it has occurred in whole grades of paper (such as newsprint).

So how, do you combat this dangerous phenomenon in your company? There are several approaches that may work. The first one is to move people around regularly and randomly. Don't let small groups develop extremely long term alliances. Another way is to invite outsiders in to offer opinions—and make it a rule that their opinions must not be dismissed out of hand.

It will be hard for you to fight small group lunacy, for humans enjoy the comfort that small, familiar groups provide. I recently participated in a survey for a major polling group that allowed one to look at the results when they were done. Something like 57% of the respondents considered comfort and a lack change to be very important, desirable attributes in their lives. Fighting this is paramount to moving your company forward at all levels.

In the area of safety, group think is just as dangerous as it is in the cockpit of an airplane. We must continually challenge the status quo if we expect to be safe.

Be safe and we will talk next week. ##

Paper or Plastic--but not what you think

Week of 8 Jun 09

Monday I was in St. Louis, talking to a group of paper machine specialists about the most important machine— the invoice printer. I spent quite a bit of time with this group stressing why specialists of any kind should be interested in the business (invoices) of their company (more below).

Tuesday evening found us in Nashville, on the porch of good friends having a delightful dinner outdoors in marvelous evening weather. The conversation turned to financing, a subject this friend and I have discovered we share much common despite him being an executive in the music industry. We found a mutual interest here several years ago in the go-go days of private equity when a company I was helping decide whether or not to buy a paper company came along and considered buying his employer in the music industry. Hey—paper or plastic (CDs) —same thing, eh?

Tuesday evening, he related a recent refinancing by a major record label. It happened just a few weeks ago. First, analysts for one of the largest Wall Street banks juiced the stock, moving it from a hold to a buy. Our executive friend said people in his industry were scratching their heads asking "What changed?" It soon became clear—this bank did a large refinance for the music company within a couple of weeks. In other words, nothing had changed—it was all about selling the deal.

The amazing thing this shows is the banks (at least this one) have not learned the lessons of the last nine months of financial upheaval—they are still up to their old tricks. Coincidentally, a couple of weeks ago, I met a retired banker that had worked on a major financing in our industry in the late 1980s. We were talking about the bonuses bankers earn today. He asked me if I had any idea what he had earned on that large deal as the lead banking professional for the lead bank. I bit and said, "How much?" His answer: $2,500 which was an unprecedented and large amount for that time.

Many companies in many industries, including, of course, ours, are burdened with financings that should not have been done and which were loaded with extraordinarily large overhead expenses. From the above recent example in the music industry, apparently these appalling techniques continue to this day.

Enough of that—it is largely out of control of the readers of Nip Impressions. I'll end with a couple of things I said to the St. Louis crowd about spinning the invoice printer. First, I acknowledged that they were a collection of specialists, typically far away from the invoice printer. However, I told them, you are not in some vast social protective net where your job goes on no matter what— in fact, if you have been paying attention at all, you already know this. You are more like the crew in the engine room of an old ship—you may seldom see daylight, but you are highly interested in what is going on on the bridge. The exogenous opportunities and threats are of great importance to your long term career well-being.

And then I really got their attention. I told them that if I were in charge of a mill and was order to cut staff, my criteria would be this: what is the unique link between each professional staff member and the invoice printer? If I can't find one, I am afraid I would have to tell you that you have to go.

We all know our links to safety. Or at least we should. If you do not, ask about them in your next safety meeting.

Be safe and we will talk next week. ##

Something to talk about...

Week of 21 Dec 09

In the coming couple of weeks, most families around the world will be gathering. These are dysfunctional times, when Uncle Silas gets a little tipsy and starts telling us all he knows and what he would do if he ruled the world. If you are my age, you have sat through decades of these "educational" events. I have discovered this phenomenon crosses cultures, religions, ethnic origins, you name it.

Anticipating these times, it occurred to me that you and I, readers of Nip Impressions, have a wonderful opportunity to (a) take control of the conversation and (b) do something positive for the industry we love. In fact, if you will do what I suggest below, we'll have a chance to influence 50,000 to 100,000 people by January 2010 in over 90 countries around the world. The math comes from the reality that Nip Impressions is delivered to over 90 countries each week and assuming (a) a modest number of you are willing to execute the plan outlined here and (b) have family gatherings of around 10 people at least.

This idea comes in two parts. Below, in many languages, are click throughs to Adobe(r) PDF files. Each file is two pages, same content different format. The content is labeled "Forest Products Facts" and is a listing of ten (10) easily verifiable positive aspects of the forest products industry. The first page is one you can print out and hang in your office or place of work, to remind you of some of the many positive aspects of our industry.

The second page is a page of multiple small versions, about the size of business cards. If you print this out and cut it up you can do many things with it. For instance, you could use it as gift tags, writing on the back, "To" and "From." Or, you could place one inside each present you give. Another thing you can do (we recognize some of you do not gather to exchange gifts) is place one at each place setting at a meal.

Now, about the translations. I know everyone is sensitive about their native tongue. I must admit that the Google translator was used to do the job. It has many flaws, including sometimes missing the little "squiggles" some of you like to put over letters. We also could not begin to cover all the languages spoken by you. Regrettably, we had to leave some out. So, apologies in advance if your language is not of proper grammar or spelling or is just plain missing. Just know the thought is there.

So, just click on the language of your choice and you will be taken to "Forest Products Facts" in a language you hopefully recognize.

If you happen to take some pictures of Uncle Silas learning about our industry, send them along and we'll try to find a place to publish them. Sent them to jthompson@taii.com with "Forest Facts" in the subject line.

And, of course, these are dangerous times. I mean family gatherings. Here in the southern United States, there is a famous joke about the "redneck's" last words (a redneck would be a good description for "Uncle Silases" everywhere). They are "Watch me do this!" Let's not have any of that. Be safe and we will talk next week. ##

Names

Week of 17 Oct 11

So AbitibiBowater announces, effective 7 Nov 11, they are changing their name to Resolute Forest Products. "We are changing our name to Resolute Forest Products to better reflect the fundamental characteristics of the Company we are today, including our determination, strength and resolve to be a profitable, sustainable organization," stated Richard Garneau, President and Chief Executive Officer. "With our competitive cost structure, diversified revenue base and strong balance sheet, we are well-positioned for the long term."

I hope it works for them, but a name change alone will not change the fundamentals of products, logistics, markets and cost structures.

Reflecting back over nearly four decades in the business, there are examples of good name changes, bad name changes and everything in between. Smart Papers did not mask the underlying product problems in that business. NewPage has turned out to be pages in bankruptcy.

Where name changes were important but not reflected in the businesses has often been hidden from public view. Over a decade ago, I was in a couple of old Champion mills that were cast off when International Paper acquired the parent company. The asset tags in the mills still said "St. Regis Paper" on them—an acquisition at least 15 years old at the time. The James River, later Fort James, mills, agglomerated over about 20 years, kept a number of old names and headquarters alive internally. This was a contributing factor to their demise—the fiefdoms were never killed. Management kept expecting the employees to rise up and become one big happy family. Reports I heard from the inside were that the walls of the fortresses just kept rising higher and higher—synergistic effects were elusive. Management became focused on turf wars and the customer, and hence, "spinning the invoice printer," was forgotten.

The most famous name disaster, at least in modern times, was the Smurfit Stone union. Not only did old names survive, they actually kept two headquarters—suburban St. Louis and Chicago. No wonder they went bankrupt. How else to explain going bankrupt in one of the two most stable product lines in pulp and paper (corrugated packaging)? Rock-Tenn had this figured out. As soon as they acquired Smurfit Stone, they killed all the names, killed all the satellite headquarters and are now in the process of moving what is left to the Rock-Tenn headquarters in Norcross, Georgia (Nip Impressions is puzzled, however, as to why the Norcross headquarters must expand at all to manage this new acquisition). There is weeping and wailing, but everyone knows who they work for now. History is just history.

Will Resolute Forest Products bring good karma to AbitibiBowater? Who knows? The key to this strategy will be the internal change—will it be enough to change attitudes, energy and objectives of the employees? The rest of the world, including suppliers and customers, could probably not care less.

From my experience, the name thing boils down to two truths. The first is this: if you acquire a company or two or more companies merge—make sure you kill the old names dead and rally the troops around the new name. It is worth every penny it costs to do this and do it quickly. The second is, if your business is in trouble for basic structural reasons and you think a name change might save it, it won't. Fundamentals are fundamentals, no matter whose name is on the door.

Regarding safety, name changes usually follow or lead upsetting conditions. Upsetting conditions takes one's mind off safety. Name changes should be a signal to step up your safety awareness.

Be safe and we will talk next week. ##

It is not complicated

In fact, nothing is complicated if you take the time to study it. I think I could explain calculus to a 6 year old if we had unlimited time and could keep their attention.

Which is really the problem.

We often talk about how complicated modern facilities, such as pulp and paper mills, are when the real issue is being interested enough to devote enough time to figuring out their processes. When we are in the earlier years of our careers, taken as a whole, the processes can be overwhelming (or at least they should be unless you have an ego the size of an elephant). However, years of chipping away at them, working all over the mill and learning the different processes should make it clearer to you.

The most dangerous people are those who have reached seniority by age but have never bothered to study processes enough to speak with knowledge. They speak with authority, due to time served, so to speak, but that authority is wrongly misplaced since they really don't have the experience.

I run into this in mills all the time. "Why do you do such and such," I ask? The answer usually follows from some legend or elder statesperson who made a blanket statement 25 years ago. I have a suggestion—why don't we search the literature and see what science tells us today? If overall knowledge is not gained, then why would we ever put in new machinery? Just maintain those nice, 1925 model paper machines.

In some cases, it is indeed hard to find improvements. It has taken 100 years to find a way to improve the Panama Canal. If construction goes according to schedule, there will be a new and improved version ready in 2014— exactly 100 years after the first one opened. Likewise with firearms—the Colt 1911 automatic pistol, you guessed, which debuted in 1911, is made in greater quantities today than ever before. Likewise with the AK-47 which came out, again, all together, 1947.

Pulp mills and paper machines are a bit different in this way—they are an agglomeration of many, many simple systems. The way we put those systems together changes with time. But they are little systems that can be understood. They are not mysterious.

So the next time someone feigns ignorance or arrogance under the banner of "it's too complicated" remember, it's not. Whatever it is, it is constructed of simple building blocks put on top of simple building blocks. Anyone can understand it, given interest and time.

For safety this week, remember safety is not complicated, either. It is when we get in a hurry, do not understand the ramifications that we get into safety trouble.

Be safe and we will talk next week. ##

The 1%ers

Here in the United States there has been a lot of talk about the "1%ers"—those in the top 1% of the income bracket. It has become a political theme.

I've always been a 1%er, but a different kind of 1%er. I have always been creative and long ago I was convinced that being creative in the pulp and paper industry is a lonely place—a 1% kind of crowd. It is a gift, a blessing and a curse. I have learned over the years that one has to be careful, temper their creativity among certain groups, for being too creative can get you labeled a kook, the first step before becoming ineffective. I have also concluded the "kook" label is a defense mechanism employed by the non-creative when they feel threatened you are going to upset the status quo.

Among pulp and paper companies, my experience also tells me the creative ones are the smaller ones, usually those privately held. These companies know they have to be innovative and nimble to compete with the larger ones who can spread their overhead further and ride the inertia of their business. Consequently, my consulting practice for the past 20 years has been disproportionately concentrated on the private companies. It is as if the behemoths look at me and say, "with our buildings full of Ph.D.'s and MBA's, what could you possibly know that we don't?" Well, maybe nothing, and it is perhaps just as well, for I would run screaming from the building just

163

filling out all the paperwork required to be a contractor for you.

This week, I am glowing in the 1%ers world where I belong. We just completed the Light Green Machine Institute Annual Conference and it was a great one. This venue is getting on its legs and gathering speakers and attendees in the creative 1% crowd. Dr. Brian Brogdon has been a great help as the new Executive Director in making this happen. Thank you, Brian.

But let's talk about the other 1%ers for a minute. You don't have to search very far to find a pulp and paper company that is in a fight for its life right now because a stockholder is demanding better performance. This demand for performance is driven by people in the disparaged (but not by me) 1%er crowd. Heck, I don't despise them, I want to join them (but they can keep some of their personal unpleasant habits)! I think these efforts though, while perhaps the only way we have to force publicly traded companies to improve their bottom line, miss the point to some extent. Here is how—such actions are reactive, not proactive.

Companies find themselves in such positions because they were not risk takers when they had the capital and market share to do so. They lacked the perspicacity, the fortitude, the willingness to take measured risks—the senior leaders were too comfortable, counting their personal days to retirement and not upholding their fiduciary duty to create and sustain an organization with a life beyond their own career. They simply do not see that as their responsibility and as a society we have not found a way to measure and reward/punish behavior in this area until it is too late and the padlock has been put on the gate.

The attitudes I have described in this column are pervasive not only in our companies, but in our support institutions surrounding the industry. Why Paperitalo Publications exist and why the Light Green Machine Institute exists are simply due to the absence of a welcome mat for radical ideas elsewhere in this industry's support organizations. Too many are too worried about not rocking the boat and getting themselves to their own retirement.

January is always the time for the Detroit Auto Show where the car companies, even when they were flat on their backs, rolled out their outlandish concept cars and new models. January is also when the huge Consumer Electronics Show occurs in Las Vegas. It says something about our own industry that the only really innovative conference is the Light Green Machine Institute Annual Conference here in Atlanta, ironically, in January. It wouldn't need to exist if the 1%ers, the other 1%ers, chose to take a few risks and stepped up to the responsibility of creating a long term viable pulp and paper industry.

For safety this week, consider that safety has both a short term and a long term component. You must be safe every day, but create a culture of safety that lives forever.

Be safe and we will talk next week. ##

Too much data?

Week of 16 Apr 12

Is it possible to have too much data? It certainly is— especially if you have no way to discern the important from the unimportant.

On a total worldwide basis, humankind's ability to transmit data increased by 231 times from 1985 until 2007. Sorting out what is valuable and necessary from such a deluge is difficult. In a paper mill, it is a no less daunting effort.

Driven by cheap computer memory, better sensors and higher speed processors, we prodigiously gather data today with the idea that we might need it to analyze a problem or prove a point. However, if it is not organized or comes at us at rate we cannot comprehend, more data may be more harmful than less data.

The senior professional and hourly people in our mills facing retirement in the next five years or so are best equipped to use today's volume of data. They gained experience in the industry in a time when we were able to make pulp or paper with much less data. They longed for more data and now they have it—and because they have a deep, basic understanding of the papermaking process, they know what data to ignore and what to use. They lap it up like a pack of foxhounds lap up water after a day on the trail.

What we must be concerned about is the future. I was in one of the last classes to be trained on the slide rule. This was good training, for it forced you to really understand the problem, for you had to manually assign the decimal point to your result. Hence you had to have a "feel" for what the answer should be.

Pulp and papermakers of the retiring generation have this "feel." They know the operating parameters for their mill that make sense. People without this understanding can look at the volumes of data thrown at them and not be able to comprehend either what is important or what is realistic. It is just piles of numbers. Lots of piles of numbers.

Lawyers use the overwhelming data approach to foil their opponents in a lawsuit. You subpoena their information and they will more than gladly dump so much information on you that it is impossible to find the needle in the haystack. Data overload works to their advantage.

The same thing that works for lawyers does not work for pulp mill operators or papermakers. We want the succinct data we need to operate today. We want the rest of it stored where we can find it should we ever need it. This is a far larger task than just providing all the data possible.

Pulp and paper companies are behind on hiring the next generation of professionals and operators. When times have been bad for the industry, they have cut costs by allowing natural attrition take its course. Today, and in the near future, we as an industry are going to pay for this as the intersection of inexperience and the flow of cheap data collide. It may not be a pretty process.

For safety this week, data on accidents may help you reduce them. Safety is still and always will be an attitude issue, but data can show you where you need to concentrate.

Be safe and we'll talk next week. ##

So, what is the definition of a successful paper mill?

Week of 18 Feb 13

For the past 25 years, I have been involved in site selection for new pulp and paper facilities. I have also been involved in shutting down a fair number of poor performing facilities.

What is your definition of a successful pulp and/or paper mill? If you are local to such a facility and work there, a big piece of it is probably steady or rising employment. If you are in senior management or an investor, it is probably something else, most likely net profits or return on investment (just ask Starboard Value LLC or Pershing Square).

As I think back over the past three decades, there are certain unchanging facts that have become quite evident in the whole business of siting and running the successful facility.

On the siting side, these conditions apply: markets, raw materials, logistics, energy and the environment (meaning a source of water and conditions favorable for permitting). Not once have I been aware of a mill, at least in the last three decades, being sited based on a supply of qualified labor. This is true anywhere in the world. Labor is never a factor in siting a mill, otherwise there would never have been a pulp mill built in Brazil, to cite an extreme example.

What causes mills to be shut down? Number one issue is markets. Look at newsprint. Market dried up, mills go out of business. Number two reason is probably a tie between energy and the environment: local energy costs too high or environmental pressures too great. Number three reason: labor. Labor conditions so unruly and unreasonable that they put the mill out of business, or are at least a factor that tips the decision significantly.

If you work in a mill, it is important that you think about these conditions. I'll repeat them. First, local labor (and, I'll add, management talent) is never a condition considered when siting a mill. Second, labor can be one of the top three conditions for closing a mill.

The question before you then, is to reconsider how these facts, for indeed they are facts, affect your view of the successful mill? Further, how do they affect your daily behavior?

On the one hand, one might see them as discouraging. For, one point of view is the best you can do is not be a factor causing the mill to shut down. On the other hand, look at the things that do cause mills to shut down. From your position, how can you influence them? How can you not only keep your mill out of the shutdown ledger, but move it toward being a roaring success for those who do have the power to say "yea" or "nay"?

Cluelessness comes at all levels. A few years ago, a banker called me in to look at a facility where they had a loan, in fact they had the first lien on the property (a powerful position). We had a meeting with the top management (who thought they were the "owner"). It started about 10 a.m. At noon, the "owner" excused himself to go have lunch with a buddy, never to return that day. By 4 p.m., I recommended to the banker that they pull the plug—the "owner" was obviously not engaged, the books were a mess, chaos reigned. They put the mill in bankruptcy almost immediately. The good news in this case is that the mill was bought out of bankruptcy and is now being successfully run (by bankers' definitions) and providing significant local employment.

For safety this week, consider that a component in the shutdown issue, or shall we say a subcomponent, is the mill's safety record. This is obviously part of the people portion of the equation. A good safety record is, indeed, part of a successful mill.

Be safe and we will talk next week. ##

Going and Coming—implications for the pulp and paper industry

Week of 25 Mar 13

Despite Yahoo CEO Marissa Mayer's decision on February 22nd to do away with the policy of working at home, I don't think this is a seismic change for businesses' long term trends. Working at home makes so much sense, both from economic and efficiency viewpoints, that Ms. Mayer will not turn around an entire trend. Granted, she has a problem she is trying to solve—Yahoo employees only generate $344,000 in revenue each per year while Google's comparative number is $930,000. But expect when she fixes that problem, she'll loosen the policy again.

So, offices, as we have predicted for a long time, will continue to go away. This has implications for several grades of paper, from copy paper to away-from-home tissue products. One could argue the good and bad for these grades several ways—I am no expert but can see both sides of the analysis (hey, I am a great consultant—"on the one hand, on the other hand"). The point is this, if you manufacture grades distributed to offices, you should continue to expect the distribution system to morph into a model that efficiently serves the home office.

Those are the obvious implications. There are others involved in the home office transformation. What happens to office grades that might be associated with commuting to work (disposable coffee cups or fast food wrappers, for instance)? Would diapers (nappies) with a moisture sensing RFID tag whose message pops up on your computer while you wordsmith that contract for your client be something that could gain traction? What else can change in paper grades here? The good news is home office dwellers tend to act more like retail consumers, and thus may be susceptible to value-added impulse buys at your local office supply big box store. Clearly, the centralized office is going away.

The other trend nearer to coming to into the realm of reality is one of which we have spoken before. It was announced this past week that an innovator/entrepreneur is planning on developing drones that can deliver packages ("drone" is the common vernacular, the official name is RPA, or Remotely Piloted Aircraft). We have been predicting this for a couple of years. The grades this will affect? Anything used in packaging. How will these grades be affected? Who knows? However, I would urge packaging grade manufacturers to get on board with these ideas.

The last go around, about 130 or 140 years ago, we let the railroads tell us how to make boxes. Hence the infamous Rule 41 which lasted well into the 1990s in some places. Want someone to lead this effort, I would suggest Randy Phares, of the Paperboard Packaging Group (and no, I have not discussed this with him—he is the obvious natural leader that comes to mind).

If there is a theme to this week, it is that the world of tomorrow is not the world of today or yesterday. If you are going to stay on top of your game, you will embrace it and be a leader, no matter your paper grade.

For safety this week, if you work in an isolated office, how do you plan for safety emergencies? What is the plan if you become incapacitated, have a heart attack or something worse while working alone? Plan now.

Be safe and we will talk next week. ##

Earplugs

Week of 29 Apr 13

When we surveyed our audience a couple of weeks ago, asking them about their opinion of the behavior of sports' talent on the day-to-day behavior of the average person, the response was large and overwhelming of the opinion that the behavior of such people, both on and off the field, is a very big influence. I think little things matter, too.

I do not have a large cache of earplugs, since I do not belong to any particular mill or operating site. It is customary that clients supply these, usually having a large supply handy at the place where one is about to go into a hearing protected area. I'll proudly tell you I am carrying around and regularly using a set of these I picked up at a client's site about 27 months ago (don't write me about the hygienic issues possible here).

Yes, they were a throwaway set, but they were slightly better than the usual ones—they came in their own plastic throwaway case. I like them. For a while, I kept them because it was handy to have them around—I could put them in their case, inside the case that holds my prescription safety glasses. Nice to keep these things together.

After a while, and I cannot tell you when, it became a matter of pride to hang on to the same pair, to see how long I could make them last and not lose them. And, as of this writing, I have been able to keep them (a bit of mental agility exercise) and preserve them in good condition.

And they have made me frugal, the point of this week's column. For I believe strongly that it is our dealing with the little things that sets the tone for dealing with the big ones. Since I have been husbanding these earplugs, I have thrown away less copy paper that ran through the machine blank. Why not save it?

I once knew a company in the Midwestern part of the United States whose specialty was earthmoving. The company had started in the 1930s and hit it big in the late 1950s when the US interstate system was developed. Their location and experience garnered them huge earthmoving contracts for many years. However, the owner and president's assistant remembered the old days. On her desk was an old fashioned adding machine— the kind with a paper tape (this was just before personal computers). If you walked into their offices, offices sitting in the middle of a one hundred acre field crowded with earth moving machinery (and, I was told there was just as much out on job sites), you would find the adding machine tape stringing out of her machine and onto the floor. Why? Because when she got done with one side of the tape, she rolled it back up and used the other side. She remembered when the company was not so well off.

Today, when I walk from a parking lot into a mill, looking down, the ground is littered with discarded earplugs.

I believe people who discard earplugs likely treat other assets, expendable or otherwise, with the same lack of appreciation of costs.

Your cost control program may be as simple as starting with ear plugs.

Of course, for safety this week, there is only one thing to talk about—hearing protection. Enforce it and your employees' grandchildren will thank you.

Be safe and we will talk next week. ##

MAT

Week of 13 May 13

We have covered some other acronyms in this column before. LOC stands for Lean, Orderly and Clean. LME stands for Legal, Moral and Ethical. This week, we want to introduce a third and state (hopefully) that if you follow all three acronyms, life will be good indeed.

MAT stands for Maintained, Accountable and Trained.

Maintain an industrial facility to the highest possible standards and it will reliably operate. This, of course, means using the appropriate tools of preventive and predictive maintenance. It also means a smoothly running procurement policy and stores inventory. Wrap this around qualified suppliers and service providers, couple it with proper scheduling and one should be in good shape.

Accountability is not a group exercise. Accountability can only be personal. One person, by name, must be accountable for each essential task or responsibility on your site. You cannot stand in front of a group of people and tell them you are going to hold them accountable for a set of tasks as a group. This will not work. You can hold one person accountable for many different tasks, of course. Just don't try to do it the other way around. Want to try me out? Just tell a group of people they are accountable for a clean and orderly control room. You will have a pigsty in a week, unless one person in that group rises up on their own and takes charge, shows leadership.

T is for Training. You can never do too much training. Training expenditures almost never reach a level of diminishing returns. Proof? When you get on an airplane, you assume the entire crew, from the cockpit to the tail, is up to date on their training. You may not think about it, but you want a pilot with 100 years of experience, 50 years old, and who just came from a week in the simulator. Again, I have never seen diminishing returns to training. Operators, maintenance, procurement, sales—I don't care what the function is—you can make money by training them more.

So, the challenge is this. If you inherit a facility where the three acronyms of three, that is LOC, LME and MAT have been ignored, it is going to cost money up front to get this place into shape. The transient can kill you while expenditures go up and results lag. So you must pick and choose your targets carefully, getting the largest results for the smallest expenditures. There are two places where you can start without a blip. Legal, Moral and Ethical can be set as policy from the beginning with no costs (and probably immediate savings). After this, the first is cleaning up. We have talked before about how to do this. The second is informal training. Maintenance or Operations, Office or Shipping Dock, you'll soon figure out who has the best grasp of the duties. Have others work alongside them and learn from them.

Do these first steps and soon you will be improving your results and you can slightly increase your expenditures to gain some more improvements. I usually suggest spending first, if you are sure you can get results, and ask forgiveness later. However, this is highly dependent on the culture and policies of your company.

But the bottom line to of all this is the three sets of initials. Understand what they really mean, apply them with dogged determination, which includes hanging tough during the transition from disaster to sanity, and you will be in control of a great destiny. You can do this.

For safety this week, can you distill your safety practices and policies to a few simple words, too?

Be safe and we will talk next week. ##

177